Global City Review

Laughing Matters

ISSUE NUMBER ELEVEN · 1999

GLOBAL CITY REVIEW
Laughing Matters
1999
NUMBER ELEVEN

Global City Review is published annually.

ALL CORRESPONDENCE SHOULD BE SENT TO:
GLOBAL CITY REVIEW
SIMON H. RIFKIND CENTER FOR THE HUMANITIES
THE CITY COLLEGE OF NEW YORK
138TH AND CONVENT AVENUE
NEW YORK, NY 10031
PLEASE INCLUDE A SASE WITH ALL MANUSCRIPTS.

GLOBAL CITY REVIEW IS DISTRIBUTED BY
CONSORTIUM BOOK SALES & DISTRIBUTION

ISBN: 1-887369-09-0

GLOBAL CITY REVIEW
IS PUBLISHED WITH THE ONGOING SUPPORT OF
THE SIMON H. RIFKIND CENTER FOR THE HUMANITIES
AT THE CITY COLLEGE OF NEW YORK.

DESIGN BY CHARLES NIX

Contents

NON-FICTION

Preface

THESE STORIES, POEMS, PLAYS, ROUTINES, COMMENTARIES, monologues are so funny and together so accurate in representing the complexities of both psyche and culture, that they speak for themselves. Not to mention that I put off writing this for so long that it's way past press time. Luckily, though, Grace Paley was also late in sending the following poem, so since we're out of space, I'm going to give my page to her.

LINSEY ABRAMS

The Poet's Occasional Alternative

by Grace Paley

I was going to write a poem
I made a pie instead it took
about the same amount of time
of course the pie was a final
draft a poem would have had some
distance to go days and weeks and
much crumpled paper
the pie already had a talking
tumbling audience among small
trucks and a fire engine on

the kitchen floor
everybody will like this pie
it will have apples and cranberries
dried apricots in it many friends
will say why in the world did you
make only one
this does not happen with poems
because of unreportable
sadness I decided to
settle this morning for a re-
sponsive eatership I do not
want to wait a week a year a
generation for the right
consumer to come along

Introduction

FROM THE FIRST LOOK AT THE OSTENSIBLE SUBJECTS of many of the pieces in "Laughing Matters"—breast cancer, an interview with a playwright whose stated goal is to end violence against women, laundry day, working as an assistant to a poet, grappling with the death of a mother, Internet surveillance, kleptomania, difficulties with Latin—there's not much that would bring even the faintest smile to one's lips. But humor is a funny thing. We found it in the freshness of the situations, the specificity of language, the familiar uprooted, the uprooted made familiar, the ability to poke fun at oneself, the deflating of self-importance in others, and, mainly, the delight in going for a laugh, no holding back. One batch of submissions after another would cause one editor to call the other on the phone and scream into the receiver with laughter, "You have to listen to this!" These stories, poems, essays, and plays and monologues demanded to be shared immediately, and we hope they provoke you, too, to dial up a friend and cackle with glee.

After the fact, the criteria for inclusion in "Laughing Matters" became clear—a case of editorial 20/20 hindsight. The work needed to be funny the first time around and it needed to be funny the fifth or sixth as well, and every time after that. As we settled in to read manuscripts, the best work, as it often does, jumped out and we knew from practically the first sentence. Other material built more slowly, kind of sidled up, threw a few elbow jabs, a few sidelong glances and before long there it was in the table of contents, confident of its place.

In this issue you'll find terrific pieces by Eve Ensler, Carolyn Ferrell, Wayne Koestenbaum, Jaime Manrique, Kate Moira

Ryan, Sarah Schulman, and many others. If anything can characterize the work here, it's a sense of the unexpected: whether it's the subject of Gerry Gomez Pearlberg's haiku, or the dating strategies in Kristin Eliasberg's "Spy Vs. Spy," or Meghan Daum's addendum to *The Rules*, or Leslie T. Sharpe's moving and hilarious tribute to her mother, we never could have predicted where these pieces would take us. The narrator in Johnnie Morello's "He Looked at Me Funny" has a unique health problem, and to say that the filmmaker in Megan Ratner's "Senso's Diary" is self-involved is putting it mildly. An interview with Eve Ensler, the author of *The Vagina Monologues* who is charting new territory in her playwriting, explores the nature of what's funny. Eve, a social activist, also talks about her evolution as an artist, and we couldn't agree with her more when she says, "Humor is revolutionary."

We've arranged "Laughing Matters" to be read straight through—the echoes between the pieces are clearer, as are the moments unto themselves. But flip it open anywhere, place a finger randomly and, well, there's no sense in assuring you that every piece will make you laugh, but you could just try it. G'wan, it won't kill you. Of course it's possible that you're a sorehead. Nah. Go ahead. Try it. Just for laughs.

BETSEY OSBORNE *and* SUSAN THOMSEN
Issue Editors

Mentor, Tormentor

by Debra Weinstein

BECAUSE I WAS EAGER AND ON SCHOLARSHIP, I WAS the student chosen to type the poems of the visiting professors. Because I was young, and maybe too hungry, they loved me the way my parents loved me—clearly, they didn't love me. Because I was weak, I had a long apprenticeship.

There are things you do and you have a vague idea while you are doing them that they are making an indelible impression. If you are grandiose, perhaps you think you will write about them in your memoirs. If you are like me, you think this is the kind of thing I'll be recalling on the couch years from now—if I ever get there. Such was the nature of my relationship with Professors T., X., and Ms. Z.

My relationship with Professors T. and X. lasted one semester. My relationship with Ms. Z. would last a lifetime. I could tell you things about Ms. Z.—the frequency of underwear to T-shirts in her laundry, but I am going to be kind.

What is poetry, I would ask myself, over and over, typing,

"*the sudden, half-chirped, pecked-hem of morning*"

or

"*my arthritic half-moon, far-reaching thought (?), spine (?)*"

And then in the margin, this note to me from Professor T., asking for advice on his poem: "Annabelle, which sounds better—" And I would think to myself, hmm, 'far-reaching thought' or 'far-reaching spine?' Hard to say.

I want to say that my own poetry suffered from this activity, but that was not the case. My own poetry was free of chirping, hems, thoughts, and spines. It would be more realistic to say that I suffered. I felt like someone who sits at the foot of the goddess simply because it seems like the right place to be at the time.

Would Gertrude Stein have licked Sappho's boots? I asked myself.

When the visiting professors left, I got another assignment. I became the personal assistant to Ms. Z. Ms. Z., how to talk about her? She inspires admiration, envy, reverence, and dread. She is award-winning, ground-breaking. She writes astonishing poems about nature. Flowers recklessly endanger other flowers, and you actually believe it. There was something I wanted to learn from Ms. Z.—

"*. . .unnatural world, whorled, begotten, petalled—*
I see you and forget desire. . ."

In our quiet moments, I would be sitting on the chair in her office, just finishing dictation, or writing down my errands, and say,

"I want to ask you a question about "whorled, begotten, petalled—" and Ms. Z., very kindly would lean forward as if she had all the time in the world, and answer me. At those times, I would learn something about how poems are made. At those moments, the mystery of creation would open up unto me.

"Well," she said, "In the poem, 'Unnatural World,' I was thinking about prostitution. Knew I had to disguise that thought! When I said, 'unnatural world, whorled, begotten, petalled,' I was really thinking, 'Unnatural world — whores begotten, peddled.' Anyway, that was the idea that inspired that poem," and then, without missing a beat, she smiled and added, "I'll see you at five o'clock."

Outside the sun in my eyes was too much. I was always shocked by my conversations with Z. Of course, I *knew* that her poems were about sex. But slowly I was beginning to understand that the drumbeat in her head was sex too.

That afternoon, in the stationery store, buying the ink cartridge for Z.'s fountain pen, I understood that I would never be a great poet. I knew this truth to be self-evident: that if ever I thought *whore*, the only word I would write would be *whore*.

There were things I did for other people. Favors I did for Z. which were actually favors for other people. I did her correspondence, and if she adored someone she would send them poems, but these were often obscure poems, poems you could only find in magazines.

I would think of this activity as the poetry hunt, and every time I got a note sending me on one, my heart would sink a little, "Annabelle, I am looking for a poem by Yvonne Miller (?) in a journal which had a very short publication life perhaps *United Poetry Journal* (?). I recall this line: 'the lark singing twer-will, twer-will...' "Then I would be lost for hours in the library, among the dark stacks, searching for a magazine. What is literature anyway, I would think looking at the students at their tables, coated with dust. I will end up here too someday, unread, dust-coated; another lost document written in the ancient hand called poetry.

Dear Henry,

Thank you so much for your letter. Your new poems are breathless! Especially "Truck Driving South" — bold, punchy, acerbic. Many hours in the library and a phone call to Austria led me to that poem by Igor Milan, 'The Lark.' Do you know it? Milan's bravado is a lot like yours. Both of you have an uncanny ability to accentuate the stillness....

And then this note at the bottom of the page, "Annabelle, for this letter to Henry Mann, could you please get some dry rose petals and set them in the envelope. Thanks!"

Then I would write back, "Okay, but don't you mean 'articulate the stillness'?"

She was lucky to have me.

Then another note: "Annabelle, please call Mrs. Van Elder and see if there is anything you can do for her—"

"Mrs. Van Elder, my name is Annabelle S. and I am the personal assistant to Ms. Z."

"Oh, yes, dear, how lovely for her to be calling me."

"She wanted to know if there was anything you needed—"

"Oh yes, dear, why thank you. Actually there is. How kind of her..."

Then I would take this list down for Z.

Mrs. Van Elder would like:

prescription catfood
black sealing wax
and someone to read her, "The Circus Animal's Desertion."

I, of course, was that someone. She liked section III read in a whisper. "Please, dear," she would say, "read even softer." And eventually I learned by heart: "Now that my ladder's gone/I must lie down where all the ladders start/In the foul rag and bone shop of the heart." Who was Mrs. Van Elder? I don't know. She didn't offer and I didn't ask. She called me Annabelle—and she was always happy to receive the little packages I brought her from Z.—but I don't think she saw me as a person really, but rather an extension of Z.'s generosity.

There were things I did for Z. that I really didn't mind doing. I would often take trips to the Botanical Gardens to catalog flowers. Then I was the research assistant on her knees examining a flower, writing a brief description and sketching the flower in a notebook. She gave me a box of one-hundred fine-point markers so I could be exact in my renderings.

"Annabelle," Z. had asked, "Who was Virginia Woolf?"

I felt embarrassed, insulted. "Was she a writer?"

"Yes, a great writer...And Virginia Woolf sometimes wrote articles. And do you know why she wrote articles?"

I said, "So she could earn money and buy a motor car with the profit."

"Actually, she bought a Persian rug with the profit—"

"But first," I said, "She had to kill The Angel in the House."

"Yes, The Angel in the House," Z. repeated slowly, wistfully. Then: "Annabelle, I am going to offer you something quite unique. You will be one of the rare poets to actually get paid for her words."

"For my typing?"

"No, for your notes. For your little descriptions of flowers, I will pay you $2.00 a page, above and beyond your salary and travel time. It will be our contract. In a sense I will be paying you for your lines."

Because I was on scholarship and financially impoverished, and because there seemed no reason to refuse, I agreed. But since the publication of *The Flower Poems*, *The Flower Psalms,* and that long epic poem, *Flower Soliloquy*, I realize I may have been too ambitious in my note-taking.

Flowering asters: each like a star, the glint in an eye, a tubular flower, yellow, pointed.

Maiden pinks: a simple flower, like a button, braided through a young girl's hair.

Wisteria: like hysteria, only it clings to a building, a bunch of purple flowers hiding a sturdy vine.

When I could, I spent my every free moment in search of the almighty flower. But like everything I did for Z., writing about flowers, too, felt onerous. And, once again, I began to question what is literature, what is poetry. I thought of Keats' "wealth of globed peonies," and knew that I would never write a line that beautiful.

Some months after I handed Z. the last page of my flower research, she was awarded the prestigious Fowler grant for work-in-progress. Then poems started to circulate with my lines and an interview was published in *Poetry: America!*

*

Interviewer: Can you talk a little about your new flower poems? I am especially interested in the "Wisteria" series. Let me quote the beginning of the title poem:

> *Little hysteria, you cling to a building—*
> *I should have jumped, disguised the thought,*
> *written about my father years ago...*

Z.: "Wisteria" grew out of my interest in hysteria. I had been reading a lot about Freud and Dora. Started thinking about the vines, the bushy flowers, etc., you know. (Cough, cough). I was trying to take on history.

Interviewer: (Laughing). In "Maiden Pink," you go back in time to 630 B.C., appropriating the voice of Sappho, or what we surmise to have been Sappho.

> *Maiden Pink*
>
> *A simple flower, like a button*
> *braided through a young girl's hair.*
> *Each star, a button*
> *braided through my daughter's hair.*

Interviewer: How do you write?

Z.: Well, I write all the time. When I am not writing, I am gathering references, researching my work. I wrote these new flower poems in a white heat. I had been collecting notes for quite some time and then it all suddenly came together and I literally did not stop until I was finished. I wrote from early morning until nine at night leaving my desk only for meals, and of course, to sleep...

She was in the prime of her writing life and I was typing her letters.

I wrote in my notebook:

> If a poet writes a great poem and nobody hears it—
> If a poet writes a great poem and nobody reads it—
> If a poet never writes—
> no trees fall, no sound.

In retrospect, I was depressed. I had lost my own desire to write, and could no longer look at Z.'s poems with awe, though I tried. Flowers, after all, are a metaphor. They hide what is ugly. One day, after dictation, I said, "Ms. Z., by the way, I'm a little broke, and am having trouble living on my stipend, and am afraid that I'm going to have to go home to live with my mother. So I have to leave my position, but wondered, could you write me a recommendation for my file?"

"Oh dear," she said, and I think the sense was more, oh my predicament, than, oh my beloved.

A week later, I got a letter.

Dear Annabelle—

I do have a new helper and she is wonderful, but she is learning, slowly, slowly, so would you mind typing your own letter?

Best, Z.

*

For a few moments I was confused. I searched the envelope and looked around for the draft of my recommendation letter. There was nothing but a blank form with her signature.

My dilemma lasted about ten minutes. I imagined myself a great writer writing the story of her life.

To Whom It May Concern:

Annabelle S. has been my student for two years and during that time she has she has proved herself to be selfless, dedicated and invaluable. She is a superb line editor who knows the difference between affect and effect; whorled and whored(!). She has a sense of timing and urgency, and can be relied upon to perform any task no matter how trivial or grand.

Annabelle S. is also a gifted, talented poet. Her poems are quiet and affecting. They gather evidences and open my heart to the true darkness of a woman's soul. Her poetry: a rare distilled flower that grows through a crack in the concrete or a lush tropical that blooms in a glass house in the city. They are efflorescent and they shine. Her voice is brazen, unique. What is a poetry, I ask, and Annabelle S.'s poems cry out and answer.

Annabelle S. is, and will always be, a credit to her sponsors, and furthermore, I believe she will make a unique contribution to the poetry of our time. I wholeheartedly recommend her for an academic position, a fellowship, grant, and for any other financial support from your Institution.

I would like to report that the money, the teaching offers, the solicitations from magazines came pouring in, but I couldn't lick the envelope.

I told myself that the world recognizes great poetry, and that eventually it would recognize me too.

I put Z's letter in the far reaches of my desk drawer in the place I had once hidden the book *Becoming a Woman* from myself.

So I was repressed, regressed, self-defeating, but at least I was moral and free of influence. I sat down to write the poem of my liberation, and, this is what I wrote:

The Rival

How long have I stood in the garden, sucking,
sucking the honey of the honeysuckle,
fingering the dusting stamen,
holding the rival's hand.

Then everything was rainbow, rainbow, rainbow, and I let the poem go...

An excerpt from

Hadley's Mistake

by Kate Moira Ryan

SCENE ONE

(Stage left is a door that says McManus Literary Detective Agency. *Cadence flicks on a desk light.)*

CADENCE: This is a story about how life can change in an instant. This a story about how a suitcase was lost. And then found. About how I lost my first wife. And then… (Beat.) This is a story about what happens when someone asks a question, buys you a drink, someone asks you to stay. This is a story about what happens when you don't walk away.

(Cadence gets up and puts on her trench coat. She flicks off the desk light.)

CADENCE: It all started at a lesbian piano bar around 3 A.M. The girls were slurring Sondheim and I was finishing my next to last drink.

(Cadence sits down at bar and sips a drink. She takes her money off the bar and counts out a tip. Another drink is slammed in front of her. The bartender nods towards the end of the bar. Tribley raises her glass. Tribley sits wearing a private school blazer with jeans and a pair of moccasins. Her left eye is bruised. There is a tattered plane ticket sticking out of her front pocket and a small suitcase by her feet.)

CADENCE: (*Lifting glass towards Tribley.*) I'm old enough to be your mother.

TRIBLEY: Well, I was never breast fed.

CADENCE: Does that turn you on, incest?

TRIBLEY: I don't know. You have to have a family to have incest. A mother or a father, siblings. It's just me. I'm a ward of the bank.

CADENCE: Where'd you get that black eye?

TRIBLEY: I walked into a door or maybe it was a fist. Whoops. (*Tribley almost falls off the barstool.*)

CADENCE: You should go home.

TRIBLEY: I start school tomorrow in Lausanne. (*Pats ticket in breast pocket.*) My flight leaves at 7 and I'm going to stay up until then. I'm trying to avoid jet lag.

CADENCE: You're going to have a lot more than jet lag.

TRIBLEY: Not if I don't go to sleep. They stay open here until 4:30.

CADENCE: You've been here before?

TRIBLEY: With my great Aunt Madeline. I used to come here with her. That's why they serve me. She used to meet her classmates from Vassar here or what was left of them. She was in the class of 1934. When *The Group* was published it was said that McCarthy, that's Mary McCarthy, based Lakey on her, but my aunt said Lakey was definitely based on Bishop. That's...

CADENCE: Elizabeth Bishop.

TRIBLEY: However, the likeness between my aunt and Lakey was undeniable and the group spent hours arguing as to who was who. One night around 3 A.M., my Aunt Madeline, with certain passages underlined, grabbed the phone behind the bar and called up McCarthy in Castine, Maine. They wound up arguing in Italian over some imagined slight which may or may not have taken place in their South Tower suite some fifty odd years ago. McCarthy ended the conversation by shouting, "The relation between life and literature is one of mutual plagiarism." Whereupon my aunt screamed, "Only if you don't have an imagination," and hung up. (*Pointing at the mirror above the bar.*) See where it's chipped there? She threw her scotch and it nicked the mirror above the bar.

CADENCE: So do you come here cruising with your great aunt?

TRIBLEY: I'm proud to say we only chased the same woman twice. When I was eight, we both fell in love with Amelia Earhart.

CADENCE: Amelia Earhart?

TRIBLEY: She was one of Aunt Madeline's many girlfriends. Looked just like her. Had that tousled hair and buck teeth. I knew it had to be her. I thought she had amnesia so every time she saw me I'd be wearing flight goggles and a long silk scarf to jolt her memory.

CADENCE: And did you?

TRIBLEY: Yes, and soon after she wound up in Silver Hill, y'know the wingnut hospital. Aunt Madeline was less than pleased. She said, "You should have been named Troubled instead of Tribley."

CADENCE: Tribley? What kind of name is that?

TRIBLEY: Equestrienne. I was named after a racehorse my aunt owned. (*Reaches down the bar and holds out her hand.*) And you are?

(*Cadence walks over to her. She shakes Tribley's hand and climbs on a bar stool next to her.*)

CADENCE: Cadence McManus.

TRIBLEY: Has a nice ring to it.

CADENCE: Given to me by my father, Longfellow. I have twin sisters named Iambic and Caesura. I'd much rather be named after a racehorse.

TRIBLEY: Lately I feel like one. Jumpy and nervous. The teachers say I have an attention deficit, that I can't focus. They say I have an undisciplined mind, that I can't complete things.

CADENCE: What makes them say that?

(*Tribley takes out a crumpled set of typewritten papers. It is heavily marked in red.*)

TRIBLEY: This paper I wrote about Mr. George Herbert, the metaphysical poet. I wrote about how I didn't trust him. You can't trust someone, let alone like them if they don't have a sense of humor. I mean listen to this line, "A heart alone is such a stone." What's funny about that? Where's the sense of humor? And my teacher said, "That's wasn't the assignment." So I told her that reductive thinking is not for minds with laser disk compatibility. (*Opens suitcase and throws the paper back in.*)

CADENCE: And she said?

TRIBLEY: An F is an F is an F. So I said to my aunt, time to transfer. She said, why don't you go where I went, Mont Choisi in Lausanne, for your final term. I said sure, but I don't speak Swiss.

CADENCE: There is no such language.

TRIBLEY: That's what she said. It's for a term and then I go to Vassar. (*Slams empty bowl on the bar.*) More nuts, s'il vous plait! So what's your story, Cadence?

CADENCE: Why do I need to have a story?

TRIBLEY: What do you do, Cadence McManus? What voodoo do you do?

CADENCE: I'm the Mickey Spillane of critical thought on the brink of tenure or expulsion.

TRIBLEY: So has the blonde come?

CADENCE: The blonde?

TRIBLEY: The one that comes in wearing the dark kerchief. Your secretary buzzes you three long buzzes. Mrs. Harrington J. Watson III would like a moment of your time. You open a bottle of scotch, put on a fresh casting of lipstick. She gets shown in. You scan the Armani. Legs for miles.

CADENCE: Don't forget the dark glasses.

TRIBLEY: Of course and tells you what she wants you to find. Money's no object. Has she come?

CADENCE: Yes. He has.

TRIBLEY: Oh, and wants you to find?

CADENCE: A suitcase.

TRIBLEY: A suitcase? (*Knocks over a glass.*)

CADENCE: Are you okay?

TRIBLEY: When I drink I start to think and it gets light and dark in here. (*Taps temple.*)

CADENCE: It's awfully easy to be hard-boiled in the daytime, but at night it's another thing.

TRIBLEY: You sure know how to turn a line around.

CADENCE: It's not my line. It's Hemingway's.

TRIBLEY: No self-respecting lesbian quotes Hemingway.

CADENCE: Janet Flanner did. She a friend of your aunt's also?

TRIBLEY: (*quietly*) No.

CADENCE: You know who she is?

TRIBLEY: Of course. She wrote the letters from Paris in *The*

New Yorker magazine during the twenties. (*Takes a long look at Cadence.*) Did you know her?

CADENCE: I met her once on Fire Island when I was in graduate school, through my mentor. I was summoned for cocktails on her deck. We listened to a radio concert, Van Cliburn pounding out Tchaikovsky, while her lover mixed cold dry martinis.

TRIBLEY: Were you nervous?

CADENCE: Of course. I was hoping she could get me an interview with the reclusive Djuna Barnes for my dissertation.

TRIBLEY: And did she?

CADENCE: No.

TRIBLEY: Why not?

CADENCE: Because the news came on and Flanner shushed me while an announcer stated that Hemingway did not die from an accidental gunshot wound as had been reported a year ago by his wife, but that he had in fact committed suicide.

TRIBLEY: I thought his suicide was common knowledge.

CADENCE: For a year it wasn't.

TRIBLEY: What did Flanner do?

CADENCE: She lit another Gauloise.

TRIBLEY: You're not going to tell me?

CADENCE: It's sad.

TRIBLEY: This is a bar.

CADENCE: This is a bar five minutes shy of last call. You need to go home. I need to go home. (*Slaps money on table.*) Take a cab home, Tribley. (*She gets up.*)

TRIBLEY: Was it the same gun?

CADENCE: The same gun?

TRIBLEY: His father shot himself and he sent for the gun. Did he use that gun?

(*Bar fades to black. Lights up. McManus Detective Agency. Ernest is in background cleaning his gun.*)

CADENCE: (*Addresses audience.*) This is the moment, the exact moment where I could have walked away…

ERNEST: But, there was the wife waiting for an answer.

CADENCE: What do you do? Do you go home with the answer that will end it? Do you go home with the answer that will save it or do you just not go home?

ERNEST: I've done all three.

CADENCE: This is the moment when I could have walked away, gone home and found that wife of mine.

ERNEST: And given her the answer.

CADENCE: But, in my profession it's best to travel alone.

ERNEST: The dames, the chippies, the wives…

CADENCE: Complicate everything. I still run the decision I made through my mind like a comb over knotted hair. What would have happened if I walked away with nothing more than a hangover?

ERNEST: What would have happened if I hadn't said,

CADENCE: No, it wasn't the same gun.

(*Ernest fades into the background. Lights up on the bar again. Cadence sits back down. Tribley waves a bill.*)

TRIBLEY: Two for the road. What did Flanner do after she lit her Gauloise?

CADENCE: After Flanner lit another Gauloise, she cleared her smoker's throat and told me about the first time she had met Ernest at the Cafe des Deux-Magots. He was sitting at a table by himself drinking a glass of Pernod wringing his fingers.

One of his pencils dropped on the floor and rolled towards Flanner. She picked it up and walked over to him with the pencil. "Here," she said. Recognizing the flat Midwestern accent, he asked her if she was an American and when she replied yes, he asked her to sit down. Something terrible had happened. Could he ask her advice? She brought her wine over to the table and this is what he said. Ernest and his first wife, Hadley, had been married for about a year. They were living in Paris. Ernest had a news assignment and was away with Lincoln Steffens. He wired Hadley to come and bring his novel he was working on. Hadley, thinking Ernest was going to work on it, packed the original manuscript and the carbons in a small suitcase. She put her luggage on the train and because she had some time before it left, she stepped off and bought herself a sandwich and some water. When she returned the suitcase was gone. No matter where she looked, she couldn't find it. It was gone. The train began to leave, and Hadley began to sob. It was an overnight train and she was still sobbing as it pulled into the station and she saw Ernest waiting for her. Seeing his wife so upset he tried to find out what was the matter. "Did someone die?" He asked. No. "Did someone hurt you?" No. He took a deep breath and then asked what he most feared, "Are you in love with someone else?" "How could you think of something so terrible as that?" she replied with a question. Then she took a breath and told him what happened on the train. We often think he was a hard man, a man who would yell and fight with his fists. But in that moment he held her in his arms, assured her that his love was still hers and said, "It doesn't matter. Please don't cry."

TRIBLEY: But, she had packed the carbons.

CADENCE: Precisely. Then Flanner paused in her story and I asked her what advice she gave to him. She said she told him to forget it. We sat in the dusk for what seemed like several minutes before she broke the silence again. "You should do it on him. Your thesis. You should." And I agreed, because it is awfully easy to be hard-boiled in the daytime, but at night it's another thing. It's quite another thing.

TRIBLEY: You're crying.

CADENCE: Yes.

TRIBLEY: Is it such a sad story?

CADENCE: Have you ever lost anyone you've loved?

TRIBLEY: (*Ignores the question.*) Have you?

CADENCE: Yes. Yes. Yes. I have.

(*Tribley puts her cigarette out. They both lean forward to kiss. Just as their lips are about to touch Tribley falls off the bar stool and passes out.*)

New Strategies in the Ongoing Struggle

by Daniel Kane

to reject Alan Alda as a muse I spent four hours pretending a pile
of logs was a spaceship.

to stop relying on Alan Alda as a sure-fire "money maker" for my
poetic career, I snuck a Sweet Tart into my girlfriend's palm,
then shuddered thinking about how it would taste to her.

to encourage people not to go "ha ha" every time I discussed my
Alan Alda sequence, I bought a toy helicopter which actu-
ally flew. Over a wall. Into a "rich people's" front yard.
Enormous bow-wows. Goodby, toy helicopter.

to convince people that not all my poems featured Alan Alda, I
decided to try my hand at swimming. Everything was ter-
rific until I looked down through my face-mask and saw 3
painted sharks at the bottom of the pool—a bottom so deep
I thought I would surely drown.

to cease writing "Alan Alda" poems during those times when I
lacked the inspiration to write poems, I sat in the middle of
a hotel walkway and spanked hundreds of ants to death
with the sole of my flip-flop.

to explore new frontiers beyond Alan Alda, I went to an airport
and waited for a plane. Everything was fine until the first

black people I had ever seen in my whole life decided to sit next to me, which made me start crying in fear and disbelief that such a thing could exist.

to finally absorb Alan Alda so that Alan Alda could be exuded, I picked up a big knife and cut a bagel. Part of my left thumb sliced off.

to try and think of other genres I could work in outside of the Alan Alda, I asked my art teacher how I could draw in such a way as to make it seem that one could look *inside* the picture (3D). But just 2D, 2D, even today.

to meditate on something, anything other than Alan Alda, I crawled out to my backyard to ponder. I got out just in time to see the neighbor's German Shepherd tearing away at Bubi, my white Persian cat.

to begin the difficult task of figuring out where to go as an artist now that the Alan Alda bit was "getting played," I told my sister I'd show her my erection for the low low price of a nickel.

to reject poetry entirely, Alan Alda and all, in favor of a more "honest" life of communal physical labor, I and a group of friends waited till Mr. Brown left the classroom. We then gathered around a table, grabbed it, and after counting 1! 2! 3! ? *threw it up in the air*!

to stop tailing that admittedly sweet Alan Alda, I put a bunch of tiny bread balls in my hair and stood stock still as fourteen pigeons pecked at my head.

Spy Vs. Spy

by Kristin Eliasberg

THIS IS A STORY ABOUT A GUY (LET'S CALL HIM "BOB"), and a girl (let's call her "me"). So I met Bob at my health club, and let me say quite forcefully that meeting someone at a health club is entirely against my principles. I am convinced that I don't actually belong there, among the women in their Lycra, that it's just by some weird fluke that I find myself doing something so absurd as working out at a health club at all. When I'm there I avert my eyes, or stare into the middle distance, avoiding all contact except for practicing my Spanish with the ladies who give out the towels. Be that as it may, I met this Bob at the health club and I'll just say in my defense that 1) it had been a long time between drinks, 2) he fit my notion of wanting to go out with a guy to whom I wouldn't have to explain that No, in fact I do not know the lyrics to any songs that are featured on Sesame Street, because by the time that show was on the air I already knew how to read, and I could count, too! For something really novel, I thought I might try going out with someone older than I am—say, a 40-year-old with gray hair. And there was Bob.

He seemed about 40, he had gray hair. Plus he was a tri-athlete, so, you know, think of the stamina. Things were moving along just fine, though I did continue to find the atmosphere of the health club (where all our meetings took place) highly anaphrodisiac, being of the mind that I don't want to know what someone looks like in basically their underwear until things have progressed to the point where we actually are in our underwear. But I managed to rise above that qualm, and even to almost ignore the extremely off-putting matter of the little sideways happy faces he put on his messages (we'd started exchanging e-mails). Maybe for once I should not be so snobby and judgmental, I told myself, though not really buying it.

At any rate, one day during one of our trackside chats, Bob mentioned that he lived in Norwalk, Connecticut. Not only that he lived there, but that he'd moved there recently from the city. This is not the sort of thing that a single person does, this is a married person thing. Very married. And though Bob had been certainly giving a convincing imitation of a single person, I began to have doubts. When next I discussed the boy situation with my friend "Kitty," what had been niggling doubts became looming ones. Though I won't deny I've been around the block a time or two, Kitty has been around a few more blocks and takes a slightly more hardened view of human nature than I, though she'd probably say "less naive." When she heard about the Norwalk thing, she didn't snort, but her expression pretty much conveyed the substance of such a noise, and when she pointed out that he'd been suggesting "lunch," as opposed to, say, a drink after work, or dinner, even ever-hopeful me had to admit, this was looking like a very married, albeit non-ring wearing ("like that means anything," as Kitty would say) guy.

When I tried all this out on my friend "George," just to get the male POV, George offered, without hesitation, the practical solution: "P-Trak." George has access in his office to many and various sophisticated bits of software (and I'm quite sure that the law firm he works for encourages employees to use company time for frivolous personal projects). "We have this program at work. If you can give me the guy's address, I can find out all the names of the other people who live with him. It's easy, then you'll just know what the deal is and you don't waste any time." P-trak (for Peopletrack) is your Big Brother nightmare come true. From the smallest bit of easily obtainable information (I called Connecticut information), Presto! all kinds of things you might not want people to know are there for the taking, laid out like some kind of buffet supper for any slightly computer-literate nosy person in the world. My serious misgivings about making this foray into the land of electronic surveillance lasted for about a second. In a matter of a few more minutes (actually a couple of days, because George had other claims on his time—intrusive paralegalities he had to see to at work). Anyway, in no time at all, George calls back. Turns out Bob, and now let's start calling him "Bob Williams," abides in Norwalk with another man named "Robert Williams." And from the dates of birth of the two men (yes, you can find that out, too), it looks like Bob is living with his Dad. I'd been right about Bob being forty (actually he's 42), while Robert was born in 1929. The remorse! Obviously, this guy is some kind of saint, I thought, moving to the suburbs from the city in order to take care of his ailing Dad. Even Kitty was moved to question just what sort of cynical jaded misanthrope she had become. "God, have I no faith in mankind?" she wailed.

Well, that clinched it. Of course now I had to go out with him, even if only to right the wrongs I felt I'd done him by imagining the worst. I was beginning to feel more than somewhat uncomfortable about my role in all this. Though the temptation of high-technology had been irresistible, it was also a little creepy. I had this knowledge I shouldn't have, and I'd been underhanded about getting it. It's a loaded time bomb when you know something about someone and there is no plausible way that you could have found it out. In these situations it's inevitable that you will mention the one thing you shouldn't. When we met for our date—and to add to my guilt, of course, he'd been quite agreeable to meeting for a drink instead of lunch—almost the first thing out of my mouth was something about his "moving back home," at which reference Bob looked quizzical, and said, "but I grew up in Ohio." "Oh, yes, of course," I said, "And you just live in Norwalk now, right?" And why the Hell do you live in Norwalk, anyway, I'm thinking, Why don't you live on the Upper West Side, like all the other single guys with good jobs? Between trying to cover up my guilty knowledge, and the nagging feeling that I shouldn't have been spying on him in the first place, and wrestling to keep my inner judgmental beast at bay (So he works for an investment bank, they can't all be assholes), it didn't look like it was going to be a stellar date. And Bob is unhelpfully drinking Perrier, which was not encouraging. Say what you will about the scourge of alcoholism, there is nothing like a drink or two to ease a tense date situation, and I, for one, could have used some easing. As if my unconscious had assumed control, the conversation kept veering round to computer technology. While pursuing banking by day, Bob, it turns out, was busily building his own business by night—creating an Internet directory of addresses, phone and fax numbers, and e-mail addresses, so that you could—guess what?—track people down! I'm trying to figure out how to tell him, without tipping my hand, that actually, such a resource kind of already exists, when things start to get even more interesting. Being a computer kind of a guy, Bob, he ruefully confesses, did an Internet search on me. "You have a sister, don't you?" he asks, almost accusingly. And he's right, I do. I have a sister whose name evidently shows up fairly frequently on the credits of various exhaustively archived television shows. I admit to having a sister, but I'm thinking that it's a pity we've missed that moment when you decide to start telling each other about your families and you get to see how someone looks when they say something like I have an older sister who works in TV—a look that I suspect in my case would speak volumes. I'm also thinking pretty poorly of his surveillance methods. No, not because he didn't use P-track—we can't all have access to amateur private eyes with boring jobs in cushy law firms—but because my name has been in the newspaper of record—I've even been in some magazines of record. Really, it seemed to me, a child with a search engine, with a library card, could have found out stuff about me.

So this is all getting pretty passing strange, and I'm kind of squirming in my seat, thinking should I tell him? Or should I maintain my illusory possession of the moral high ground? when, while we were on the subject of confessions, and some of you may have guessed this by now, Bob tells me that, in fact, he is married, though admittedly not currently living with his wife. ("We were going to get a divorce but there's been too much going on this year, so something had to give. We're going to wait till next year.") I'm kind of kicking myself, and thinking, you idiot, and but also feeling kind of relieved—now I don't have to go out with him. And I'm also dying to ask: "So what about the old geezer guy who's listed at your address, what's up with that?" But I never did find out, as my rule about married men is right up there with, but even much more strictly enforced than, my rule about guys you meet at the health club. So that was that. (That was even more that when, the next day, Bob sent me a message filled with admiring comments about myself and my person that made me uncomfortable way beyond the range of my usual "I don't like compliments" discomfort. There was nothing lewd or anything, more along the lines of, "Boy, what a pleasure to meet a woman who has a mind of her own and great legs." As George put it, "the only thing like that it's O.K. to say to someone you haven't slept with is the one about 'good posture,' and even that. . ..")

Since then, I've abandoned my experiments with high-tech surveillance. Clearly it's not worth the guilty feelings—besides which half the information you're going to get is probably false and/or obsolete. But I've also abandoned my "target" approach to dating. So Bob was older than I was and had gray hair and, presumably, lots of stamina. So what? He wasn't plausible in any way BUT statistically. The next guy I went out with definitely did not have gray hair, and if he lived with someone born in 1929 it was his grandfather. But somehow he was plausible—we got along, he knew people that I knew, we met in a bar (far more congenial than at the health club with George Michael blaring), and he drank beer and he didn't use little sideways smiling faces on his e-mails. So I couldn't see him on weekdays if he had homework, so you can't have everything.

How will you know when it's done?

by Robert Danberg

Sniff the steam. Rice blooms in steam.
Popping means the water's gone.

Add the tart part last. Taste as you go.

Prick the thickest part of the thigh.
If the juice runs clear, it's done.

When a toothpick comes out clean,
and it springs to the touch.

When the consistency is that of whipped cream.

If you drop it in cold water,
and can form a ball.

Translucent.

Golden brown.

Reduced by a third.

Doubled. Tripled.

When it forms soft peaks.

Hannah's Boy

from *Life Has Many Roses: A Daughter's Memoir*

by Leslie T. Sharpe

BOZO IS SITTING ON MY LAP.

"That dratted cat," I can hear my mother say. "He won't let me do anything."

Bozo jumps from my lap to the desk, insinuates himself around the computer keyboard, then rests his chin on the function keys. The monitor screen twitters.

"Everywhere I am, he has to be," she complains. "If I try to work, he sits on my papers."

"Mother, if you really wanted to work, you would."

"Don't talk to your mother that way."

"Look," I say, exasperated. "Just throw him off the table."

"I can't!"

"Why not?"

"Because he won't let me."

Gently, I lift Bozo's chin from the keyboard. Just as gently, he replaces it. "Bozo!" I say, trying to sound stern.

He starts to purr, opens his amber eyes, deep with understanding. "Bozo with the tear in his eye," my mother called him, in deference to the drop of tawny gray on his otherwise white face.

I guess I can always work a little later.

* * *

My mother loved to complain. She enjoyed it thoroughly, as she did everything in her life. My mother complained passionately, with conviction and admirable sincerity. She was a principled complainer and a loving one. She only complained about those she truly cared for.

Mother complained about Bozo a lot. She also worried about him. Worrying was the true test of my mother's affection. If she worried about you, it meant you were family. And family to my mother was everything.

In the end, Bozo was my mother's family. I was too, of course, but I lived in New York City, and my mother was in the Philadelphia suburbs, where I had been born and raised. He was her constant companion, the recipient of her sharp, generous love. "Drat that cat," she would grumble. "I can't go anywhere since *he* showed up." She did allow herself to visit me in New York, especially at Christmas, and she spent that last Christmas before she got sick worrying about both of us.

"Where are you going?" It is more of an accusation than a question.

"To the store," I answer. "You said we needed milk."

"Is it safe?"

"It's four o'clock in the afternoon!"

"People get killed in the afternoon all the time—*and* raped."

"Mother, I have to live."

"Oh don't be so melodramatic."

"Then *you* don't be so unreasonable."

"I'm unreasonable because I don't want you to be murdered? Now, *that's* unreasonable."

My mother's logic was irrefutable: The world is a dangerous place. It conspires, along with time, to take away your children. They can be snatched, sold into white slavery, or, most dangerous of all, they can fall in love.

Bozo was my mother's ideal child. Food compelled his return, guaranteed his devotion. He arrived one day at my mother's back door, a weary traveler of indeterminate age, scarred and starving.

"I don't need another cat," she told me over the phone.

"Then don't feed him."

"I already have."

"Why?"

"Because he was hungry!"

My mother fed the crows that flocked to her backyard ("They made such a racket, I had no choice."), then worried that crumbs would attract rats from Wissahickon creek, a half mile away. Mother loved the crows, clever and garrulous like herself, made acquiescent in their insolence by her gifts of bacon fat and stale bread. Food was the way my mother connected with the world. It was the antidote to her loneliness, her talisman against ills, real and imagined, the seal of her love.

Even after her first bout with cancer, when she was debilitated and often in pain, Mother insisted on sending me "care packages." Her bounty arrived in cardboard boxes that had been taped and re-taped to prevent "some stranger" from opening them. When I finally managed to cut my way through to the contents, I found an assemblage of items that might include a box of Whitman's Sampler, generic macaroni and cheese, various cans of Campbell's soups, especially her favorite, consommé, stale Girl Scout cookies, and a "wrinkle-resistant rayon slip."

In the box I would also find a jar or a tin with a label marked FROM HANNAH'S KITCHEN. These were treats my mother made herself, exotic, subtle chutneys, party mix concocted from a recipe on a cereal box, sweet, slightly singed meringues. If I indicated I liked any of these, Mother would deluge me with more, thrilled she had finally pleased her difficult daughter. Most of the other stuff I threw away, which I never told her, understanding as I did the significance of these tokens. Only once did I balk, when Mother shipped me the entire contents of her freezer.

John, my UPS deliveryman, arrived at my door, pale in his brown uniform, with a malodorous box that was leaking profusely. "It's from your mother," he said, stunned, unburdened his hand truck and retreated.

My mother could never part with anything, unless she gave it to me. That was her way of throwing things out.

"Just stick it in the freezer," she said, when I called to complain and urge her not to send such a package again.

"You can't refreeze food that's been frozen."

"Are you sure it's thawed?"

"Mother, the stuff is sopping wet!"

"Well, you can't waste it."

"Then what am I supposed to do?"

"Eat everything now," she suggested. "Have it for dinner."

My mother's generosity was often overwhelming and always indiscriminate. In that package were two slabs of scrapple, "a Philadelphia tradition," according to the wrapper. To my mother scrapple meant home, and when I visited, invariably I would find on my breakfast plate several slices, cooked to a seductive crispness.

"Mother, you know I don't eat scrapple," the conversation would begin.

"Why?" she'd ask, feigning innocence.

"It's fried pork scraps!" I'd erupt.

"And cornmeal," she'd counter. "That's healthy."

"I don't want any, all right?"

"Oh have some, for heaven's sake. The crown won't fall off your head."

"I just don't like it," I'd lie.

"You used to love scrapple, when you were a little girl."

"I'm not a child anymore. I'm an adult."

"Then act like one and eat your scrapple."

"You eat it."

"But I made it for you!"

This was a recurrent skirmish in the battle of our wills. To refuse my mother's food was to cut a cord between us. My struggle was not just to become independent—it was to be separate.

"Bozo likes scrapple," Mother announced over the telephone.

"Who's Bozo?" I asked, just to annoy her, since I knew full well my latest sibling's name.

"My new cat," she said indignantly. "My Scottish fold."

"Mother, that is not a Scottish fold."

"Then what is he?"

"An old tom with torn ears," I said crankily.

"Well," she said, triumphant, "at least he's smart enough to know what's good for him."

Bozo was my mother's last cat. When I was growing up, we had lots of cats, and dogs, and birds, and fish, and even an alligator, which my big sister brought me from Florida, a surly souvenir of spring break when she was in college. My father wanted to ban the traumatized critter. But mother protested it was just a baby, and though conceding that it was good for nothing and stank, allowed me to keep it. Her tolerance was soon rewarded by the reptile's untimely death. I found Madras, inert and desiccated, in a clot of dust under my bed, where our cat had no doubt dragged it from the makeshift aquarium on the windowsill of my room. Mother was relieved but sympathetic. She allowed me to bury the alligator in the backyard and at the internment offered this prayer: "Bless, O Lord, Your servant Madras, who left home and broke her poor mother's heart."

My mother was not a sentimental woman. When her beloved canary Dickey-bird died, she unceremoniously flushed him down the toilet, assuring me that it was a "proper Christian burial." But she suffered children everything, even allowing Ike and Dick, my pair of Java finches, to fly around the kitchen and roost in a shoebox atop the kitchen cupboard. There *was* a cage, but the birds really only used it to feed. The rest of the time they ceded it to the cat, who squeezed into the cage and sat there contentedly, rubbing his chin against the cuttlebone and watching Ike and Dick dive-bomb my mother as she did the dishes.

My mother's forbearance for the birds was finally tried when I started to write them letters. I had been banished for two weeks to a summer camp in the Poconos for "gifted children," according to the flyer, that offered "individual instruction in art and music as well as healthful outdoor activities." I was ten years old, away from home for the first time, and miserable, tortured by the violin and the tales of menstruation whispered in the dark by my cabin mates. In turn, I tormented my mother, calling her every night and crying into the telephone. Galvanized by my claim that the camp rice tasted like Clorox, Mother drove to the Poconos that weekend, resolved to take me home. Of course, by the time she arrived I had completely adjusted and announced I never wanted to go home, which made my mother cry as she left.

My phone calls stopped, but I kept writing the birds, who

had been my confidants from the beginning. I was afraid that if I stopped, I would hurt their feelings, a consideration that never entered my mind where my parents where concerned. I missed the birds and told them so in my letters, but to no avail. When I got home, Ike and Dick were gone. "You're too old to be writing letters to birds," my mother said by way of explaining their sudden disappearance, then added: "Besides, they were getting to be a health hazard."

My mother loved animals because they returned her love with the singular devotion that she craved. We always had dachshunds, a breed my mother prized for their "family loyalty," and as I grew up and edged away from her toward my own life, my stricken mother would complain, "The dog has more family loyalty than you do." The first in the line was Rudolph, a stalwart red with a deep chest and a swagger that was well earned. He had saved me when I was small from a Doberman pinscher intent on having me as a snack. Hurling himself at the onrushing beast, he so startled the dog that the Doberman turned tail—with Rudolph attached to it. Screaming, my mother scooped me up and grabbed Rudolph, all the while engaged in a struggle not only to protect her child and save her dog but to preserve her modesty, as the tie straps of her light summer shift had come undone, threatening the maternal bosom with imminent exposure.

My father would pale as she retold this part of the story, which was often in his presence, and when she started her harangue against that "good-for-nothing G.D. man" who "stood around waiting for the show to start" as her dress clung precariously to her chest, he would offer his usual discreet protest: "Hannah, please." "Oh Arthur, don't be such a coward," mother would snap, her standard response to most of my father's observations, then resume her praise of "brave Rudolph."

Rudolph was clearly my mother's dog. His defense of me, the inept runt of the litter, was limited to attacks by outsiders. In his own territory he kept me at bay, growling when I tried to approach mother as she lay in bed, ever vigilant by her side. Rudolph guarded her with the same fierce jealousy that she protected us. My sister, who craved my mother's love as much as she was repelled by it, once charged: "You love Rudolph more than you love us!" Mother recounted that story often throughout the years. "Your sister thought I loved Rudolph more than you girls. Can you imagine?"

All of our dachshunds were named Rudolph, with the exception of Sophie, a little red female whom mother would enjoin to "act like a dog, not like a worm," as she wiggled her way across the room to greet us. As per royalty, the "Rudolphs" were differentiated by ordinal numbers, Rudolph the First, Rudolph the Second, Rudolph the Third. Each dog did have his own pedigree name, which we never actually used but which my father especially took quite seriously as he was very proud of our family crest and believed that every aristocrat, even of the canine variety, deserved his due. He always picked names he deemed "appropriate," ones that reflected our family heritage as well as the dog's lineage. Thus, Rudolph the Second, a brawny black and tan, was dubbed Charlemagne of High Haven (High Haven being the kennel name) in deference both to the dachshund's Teutonic origins and my father's putative ancestor. My mother, ever practical and to the point, offered "Boom-Boom Boy of High Haven," a reference to the poor dog's unfortunate tendency to flatulence, which did not win the day, even after she emended her suggestion to "Emperor Boom-Boom."

"It was easier, don't you think?" said mother, when I asked her why our dachshunds had been Rudolphs and our black and white "tuxedo" tomcats were all Charlies. Then she sighed: "Hannah's such a beautiful name. That's what I should have called you girls."

In fact, my mother did call me Hannah. Every chance she got, she would exchange the first letter of my middle name, T (for Tansley, a "proper family name," according to my father), for H (as in Hannah, which meant "charming and gracious," according to my mother.) The gold initial pin, that token of coming of age when I was growing up in Chestnut Hill, Philadelphia, arrived on my fifteenth birthday with an H prominently emblazoned on it, flanked by an L and an S that were so small as to be barely legible. The longed-for monogram sweater, "just like your sister's," arrived similarly adorned, and in a final assault on my dignity, when I was eighteen she insisted that we share the same passport for our trip to Europe and in it recorded my name as "Leslie Hannah Sharpe" for the entire Western world (or at least every persnickety customs agent) to see.

I resisted these incursions on my identity the only way I could, by refusing to wear the pin and the sweater that I had coveted for so long. My mother's complaint that I was "cutting off my nose to spite my face" was, of course, true, but that ornate H on the very items that promised adulthood seemed like a brand that made me hers. Years later, when I would receive letters and packages purposely inscribed with "Leslie T. Sharpe" in my mother's open, expansive hand, I would reflect on what our relationship had become, a stand-off between two strong women marked by affection and respect, and I was always sure to address any correspondence to her "Hannah B. Sharpe," the "B for Browne—that's Browne with an 'e'—my maiden name," as she put it.

My mother understood the power of names, that they are markers of our individuality. But to her they were also boundaries that separate us, barriers to her all-subsuming love. "You're just like your sister," she would insist when I was growing up, despite my protests to the contrary. That denial of any difference between us no doubt made it easier for her to deny that we were separate from her. All of us—cats, dogs, and kids—mother saw as extensions of herself.

Even after she had ceded me some territory of my own, she still enjoyed skirmishing on its borders. When I told her I had gotten my own cat, after several years of living in New York, she reacted predictably: "Why do you need a cat? You've got a perfectly good cat and dog at home." When I reminded her that I no longer lived at home, she replied: "Well, you're not going to live there forever, are you?" ("Home" would always be Philadelphia; New York, that dirty, dangerous place that had stolen her daughter, was "there.") I knew my mother would take my adopting a kitten as starting my own family and I had dreaded telling her. But even when she was hurt, my mother was sharp and unrelenting. Her defense was to attack, to wear you away until you did what she wanted. My father readily forfeited small battles to her, believing, however mistakenly, that he was in control.

Sophie was my parents' last dog together, the replacement for their daughters long gone from home. My father named her Lena, which my mother immediately amended to Sophie. After a brief reign as Sophie-Lena, "Queen Sophia," as she was listed on her papers, became simply Sophie. My mother used the same tactics on me, renaming every cat I ever owned.

"Look," she'd say, triumphant, "she comes when I call her Lucy."

"Her name's not Lucy," I'd snap, glaring at the traitorous feline.

"What is it?"

"Mother, you know perfectly well what her name is. It's Fatty."

"Fatty's a terrible name for a cat, especially one that's so skinny."

"She used to be fat."

"So did you. How would you like it if I had called you Fatty?"

"Doesn't he look like a Bozo?" Mother would laugh, as delighted by the name as by Bozo himself. "Such a pretty boy."

He was an old prizefighter of a cat, the cut in the fur under one squinty eye a badge of his former profession. There was a nick in his nose, an inelegant dueling scar, and assorted bumps all over his body, no doubt souvenirs of past battles. His white fur, matted and gray when he first moved in with Mother, never learned to obey her brushing. Instead of lying down, it stood up in spiky patches, giving him an appearance that was oddly reminiscent of a stegosaurus. My mother, always loyal to those she loved, insisted that Bozo looked like a lion. "See, that's his mane," she would say of the stubby ruff that framed his pugilist's face. But it was his ears that set Bozo apart, that marked him as both survivor and champion.

Chances are raccoons had claimed them in some long-ago squabble over a trashcan. But Mother was adamant. "A pervert cut off his ears with a pair of scissors." As I would learn, Bozo's ears, or the lack of them, served to focus attention on his face, in particular his eyes, and how they searched your own. But a cat without ears set in a face as fierce as Bozo's could cause considerable consternation.

"Something's terrorizing my dog, I don't know what it is," a distraught neighbor warned my mother. "Last night it looked in the window. It has a white face, yellow eyes and no ears. It must be a devil!"

My mother's response was to the point. "That's no devil, you stupid man. That's my cat!"

Bozo was a feral cat. He had probably never had a home or had wandered off years ago to find his fortune. His scars bespoke Achilles, the epic warrior. But he had survived as Odysseus had, through cunning and deception. He tricked my mother into thinking he was the neighbor's cat. She regularly put out food for the diminutive tabby next door that she was convinced was so small because "those people aren't feeding her enough." The next morning, when she spied the inevitably empty bowl, she'd shake her head. "Why people like that have pets I'll never know." Mother didn't stop fretting, especially when it seemed the cat wasn't gaining weight.

"That cat has a worm," she told me over the phone. "Do you think I should take her to the vet?"

"Mother," I said, "she doesn't belong to you."

"That's why I like her," Mother said matter-of-factly. "She's not my responsibility."

By then my mother admitted to being "around seventy." She needed "another cat like I need a hole in my head." What she did need was to worry and complain, which she could always do about me. But she also needed to be needed, and the "neglected" neighborhood animals that flocked to her door—all in various stages of starvation, according to Mother—allowed her to love "with a minimum of fuss and bother." She didn't want a pet of her own because she was afraid it would keep her tied down to "this dratted house"—a house that, I knew, she had no intention of leaving anyway.

So when she caught sight of "some old bum" stealing from the offertory plate she devotedly put out every day, mother was adamant.

"I'm not feeding any stray," she announced over the phone.

"You don't have to."

"I don't care what you say."

"I didn't say anything!"

"If I feed him, I'll never get rid of him"—she sighed—"and I'll never go anywhere."

"You're right."

"That's easy for you to say."

"What did I say?"

"I know you want me to feed him."

"Mother, I just want you to do what you want to do."

"I don't want to feed him."

"Fine, I don't want you to feed him either."

"You don't? With winter just around the corner?"

Mother's compromise was not to let Bozo inside the house. As Bozo had no intention of being lured into the lair of any human, such an arrangement suited him perfectly. He would show up at dawn, an apparition in the half-light, a gray ghost that dissolved at the slightest sound. "He looks tough but he's really afraid," Mother reported. There was no end to the tortures she imagined he had endured, starting with his ears. Bozo stirred in my mother her fiercest love—her impassioned protectiveness. For his part, Bozo seemed to sense he had found an ally and was soon responding to her whistle as if it were a siren song. But this was no trick of the gods, no false haven. Bozo, the weary traveler, was home. He had found his Ithaca at last.

Soon "King Bozo," as my mother's friends called him, had

taken up residence in several palaces she had erected in the backyard. As the weather changed, becoming cold and raw, mother decided that the cat needed some sort of shelter. She excavated the garage, so crammed with family relics that the car could barely squeeze into it, and discovered "treasures" she readily adapted for Bozo's use, even though they were "really too good to put outside." An antediluvian kitchen cabinet, its metal compartments lined with blankets, became a duplex for His Majesty. Because "wood is warmer," mother dragged a battered old bureau out into the yard, then stuffed its drawers with sweaters purchased "for just such an emergency" at the St. Paul's Church Rummage Sale. "To give Bozo a change," she salvaged a steamer trunk and some feather pillows, in mothballs since the year one, and left the lot under the weeping willow tree, where, when he was "The Stray," mother had observed him "loitering" in warmer weather. Any number of other items soon found their way into the backyard, from brown paper shopping bags to a scratched Scotch Kooler that, for me, triggered memories of contentious family outings and having to "hold it" in the car "just a little longer."

As Bozo's "houses" proliferated, in an increasingly haphazard arrangement, I grew more and more concerned. After all, this was a discreet suburban street of pristine lawns and carefully tended gardens.

"Mother, don't you think people are going to wonder?"

"You live in Greenwich Village and you care what the neighbors think?" she countered.

"Look," I said, "it's starting to look like a homeless person lives out back."

"Makes sense," she said, after considering for a moment. "He's a homeless cat."

*

From the beginning, it was Mother and Bozo against the world. She was his patron and protector, Athena to Bozo's Odysseus. He repaid her devotion with a singular loyalty. He existed only for her. To everyone else Bozo was a phantom. "Does Hannah really have a cat?" a friend of my mother's asked me. He appeared only to her, first for food, then for affection, suffering the touch of her hand alone. He was wary for a while, which mother understood. "He's afraid I'm going to kill him," she said matter-of-factly. But she respected his caution, agreeing that trust is rarely deserved and too readily given. His experience of the world confirmed her suspicions of it, and that was a bond between them.

Bozo was my mother's cat and hers alone. He did not transfer his trust in her to anyone else. Even after he had "forced his way" into her house, he was wild. I could glimpse him only at a distance. Any attempt on my part to approach him, or simply the sound of my voice, made him scatter. Sometimes when I visited my mother, I had the sense that the house was haunted. I would catch something out of the corner of my eye, hear a creak behind me. And often I had a feeling of being watched. "He's just shy," mother would laugh. "Give him a chance to get to know you."

Mother delighted in his need for her, the exclusivity of his trust. "I'm all that he has," she would say, pity in her voice. She felt for him out of her own loneliness, her own sense of being abandoned, by her husband, who had died, by her daughters, who had left long ago. Mother admired his stoicism as well. "That old man's been through a lot," she'd say, shaking her head. She understood his suffering, even loved him for it. She herself had suffered so much . . .

*

A devastating automobile accident, when I was ten. My mother thrown from the "death seat" through the windshield. A call to my father: "Your wife is dead on Germantown Avenue." My sister saw the wreckage, unaware. A car crushed by a trolley, racing to beat a light.

"Your mother's been in an accident," my father told me.

I was standing on the stairs, gripping the banister. "When will she be home?" I asked.

"In a week," he said, not looking at me, on his way to the hospital.

It was months before Mother came home. When she did, she was bed-ridden. Her pelvis had been shattered. She would not walk for a year.

I used to bring her tea and toast. She always remembered that.

A fractured skull gave her severe headaches. She never complained about pain, but I knew. Her brown eyes would glitter black. They became hard, angry. That terrified me.

Once I tried to offer her my Sunday School wisdom, as an antidote to her suffering. "Have you tried putting your faith in God?" I began.

"Oh, Leslie, please," she said sharply.

Mother believed in life. Her faith was in the here and now, in what she could see, touch, and grasp. Life was all she had, all anybody had. It was a knowledge that made her frank and startlingly unsentimental. When she was well enough to read, she insisted on reviewing the sympathy cards that had arrived at the time of her "death." "Sorry, dear," she'd say, whenever she came across a black-bordered calling card bearing a woman's name, one of a "horde of females" that had "shamelessly pursued" my father, "but I'm still kicking."

Mother had thwarted death as she had "those damn divorcées." The latter she would have found more dangerous. My mother was concerned only with life. She had no relationship with death, despite her intimacy with it. She had lain unconscious for weeks. Sleep, the twin brother of death, Homer called it. When she recovered, she asked for her children. "I had to live, I had you girls," she would say. My mother had to survive so she did. Her will was that strong, that simple.

"Your father," my mother would say, resigned, "just isn't a fighter."

"Your mother," my father would say, resigned, "fights with everyone."

My mother fought with salesladies, argued with friends, contradicted all of us. "No," she'd say, in response to a point I'd just made, then proceed to say the same thing in only slightly different words.

"Mother," I'd protest, "that's exactly what I just said."

"Good," she'd say, "I'm glad you agree with me."

I always remembered my mother as contentious. "Vinegary," was how a friend described her after she was gone. But mother claimed she wasn't always that way. "I used to be so sweet," she'd say with a sigh, almost nostalgically. Then she'd laugh. "That's before I got smart and starting sticking up for myself." It was the accident that changed her, she said, that made her "stop taking people's guff—especially your father's."

The experience left her hard, unsympathetic. She was not a tender woman although she was a deeply loving one. She had fought to survive. She had fought and she had won. "You've got to be a fighter," she told me again and again. That was the urgent lesson she had learned, the lesson that she tried to teach me, her soft daughter, who didn't have the heart to play in a field hockey game against a friend when she transferred to another school.

My mother loved crowds. "Just look at all the people!" she'd say with awe and delight at the local mall, where I was forced to go soon after I arrived home for a visit. She loved the hustle-bustle, the clatter, the din, the lights. "Isn't it exciting?" she'd say, dragging me, exhausted, from store to store. She loved meeting new people, loved the quick and easy intimacy she could have with strangers. "That color doesn't do a thing for you," she would say to a startled shopper modeling a dress for a confused husband. Sometimes she offended people (which left her undaunted and slightly indignant), but more often than not, people were charmed by her candor. If her frankness did spark a "debate," as she demurely called it, so much the better. She enjoyed rubbing up against people—and rubbing them the wrong way. When she was arguing, she was engaged, alive, and so powerful. "You can't win with your mother," my exhausted father would say. For her, there was no such thing as "discourse." There was only life and death, victory and defeat.

By her own admission, my mother was a "fighter not a philosopher." She believed that thinking was for "people with lots of time on their hands, like janitors." In the months after her accident, Mother had lots of time on her hands. She lay in bed unable to read or even to listen to the radio. Sometimes she cried, as much in frustration as in pain. I would enter her room and sit by her bed, afraid, if she was asleep, that she might not wake up. I would will her to open her eyes, and when she did, she would lie there, so still. Years later, she told me that she only had two thoughts during that time. When she was in the hospital, she thought: "I must live for my children." When she came home, she thought: "I will walk again."

When she was recovered enough to walk on her own, one of the first things she did was to take a stroll through Chestnut Hill. "I heard the birds singing, the children playing," she told me much later, "and I realized that if I had died, all this would have gone on without me." It would be years before I understood the cruelty and comfort implicit in those words. At the time I thought my mother's insight was obvious, even clichéd. "Life goes on." Doesn't everybody know that? What I could not appreciate was that she had grasped—and accepted—her own mortality. It wasn't until I had lost her, my indomitable, indestructible mother, that I realized these things for myself.

My mother was not a religious woman. "Your father's the holy one," she'd say offhandedly. When a favorite feline died under anesthesia, the vet tried to hand her a pamphlet titled "Pray for Your Cat." "I don't want to pray," she snapped, tossing it back at him, "I want my cat." What my mother wanted was the truth. Religion, with its "song and dance," was fine for some people. But Mother was strong enough to take life—and death—on their own terms. And she did not shy away from the indelicacies of either. "Oh stop it, Molly," she'd scold her old friend ("nutty but from a good family") whenever she raised her piteous lament, "I'm so alone, I'm so alone," "How can you be alone when I'm with you?" When Molly was left alone, abandoned by her children in a nursing home "after they snatched her money," it was Mother who wiped the urine off the floor of her room with paper towels. She cleaned her and changed her, enraged at the her friend's loss of dignity, that she should end in "such crap." My mother was not given to sentiment—or to euphemism. She wrote me about the death of Sophie, the little dachshund who died less than a year after my father, leaving mother "entirely alone": "Blood came out of her nose, BM came out of her rear end, and poor old Sophie breathed her last."

* * *

Bozo has taken to sleeping on my desk chair. I come home to find its blue cloth seat cushion thick with his fine white hair.

"Everywhere I am, he *has to be."*

I attempt to remove the hair as Bozo watches. But despite my best efforts, first with hand vac, then with tape, a residue of soft fur remains. Secretly I suspect a plot. If I can't sit down, how can I work?

"That dratted cat. He won't let me do anything."

Suddenly he jumps onto the chair, curling himself into an expansive horseshoe that leaves no room for anyone else. But I am not deterred. I squeeze in beside him, utterly incapable of removing him, still my mother's soft daughter.

She would scold me for letting him up on the furniture, though she herself could not keep him off of her own bed. He also appropriated an antique wingback chair as a scratching post, ignoring my mother's protestations as another monarch, Rudolph the First, had years before, when he gnawed on the chair's wood feet, leaving tooth marks that transcended any attempt at refinishing. So Mother would have understood—though she never would have admitted as much—how Bozo has come to rule the roost in my apartment, having graciously exchanged his country kingdom for a window on a Greenwich Village street.

My mother was right about him, as she was right about so

many things. He's a sweet old man, still fearful, wary of strong voices and heavy feet. He bonded with me only out of necessity, when Mother was no longer there, risked everything for love. He is unfailingly affectionate and generous with his fur, patting me on the arm with a paw, beseeching me for attention with his yellow eyes. Those eyes . . .

"Have you ever looked into his eyes?" a friend asked recently, clearly startled.

"Sure," I said. "Why?"

"That's not a cat in there," he said. "I don't know what it is, but it's not a cat. Something else is going on in there."

Is he an old soul, as I like to think, or, as another friend suggested, unaware of any slight, a dog trapped in a cat's body? I look into his eyes and try to fathom his past. One day he simply appeared, a fragile, insistent spirit, sent to care for my mother and to comfort me.

Mother would have laughed at any such notion. "He's an old bum," I can hear her say. "A *lucky* old bum."

Mother loved a fighter as much as she loved a fight. Bozo had been tested and had won. He was a survivor, as she was. Theirs was a secret society of suffering—and of hope.

"Drat these stockings." Mother is sitting on the edge of her bed, struggling to pull on the support hose that protect legs riddled with phlebitis and, as she put it, "antiquity." I am standing in the hallway outside of her room, unseen by both Mother and Bozo, who would bolt at the sight of me. He is sitting atop a pile of rumpled bedclothes, madly kneading a white blanket with faded red roses that I remember from my childhood. He is purring loudly and patting my mother with a paw, who sits with her back to him. "Don't bother me now, Bozo. Can't you see I'm busy?" she chides, undeterred from the task that has begun virtually every day of her life for the past thirty years.

She is only partially clothed. I can clearly see the deep scar that runs over her right knee, marking the painful and difficult surgery that replaced battered bone with artificial joint. Another scar begins over her left breast and disappears into the fortress of her bra, a souvenir of yet another invasion. The scar that demarcates her recent surgery for colon cancer is a livid swath that starts under her rib cage and seemingly has no end. Her body is, as she has so often described it, a "battlefield." Earless, snaggle-toothed Bozo, his rheumy purr punctuated by coughs and sneezes, seems her perfect companion.

I am so moved by the sight of them, overcome by such a tender affection. She has been through so much, endured so much. Yet she still finds the strength to pull on her stockings, having rousted me out of bed to go to the mall.

"Leslie, what are you doing?"

"I'm getting ready," I say, slipping into the bathroom.

"You're not washing your hair, are you? I don't want you going out into the cold with a wet head."

"I'm just going to take a shower."

"Well, hurry up. Time's awastin'."

"Oh Mother, what's the rush?"

"Life doesn't wait for anyone," she calls from her room, "and neither do the best sales."

[Untitled]

by Diane Raintree

two tall ginkgo trees
waving their little green fans—
too hot to talk

Heavens to Mergatroid!

by Gerry Gomez Pearlberg

I have tried to find you, searched for you everywhere
like a sailor whose faith has left him, scanning
the horizon for a familiar star or sign.

In the unmarked grave
between merganser and merge
lies a vacant slot that should by rights define you.

Who or what are you, Mergatroid?

My sole memory of you:
I Love Lucy, the late '50s.
Someone—is it Ethel?—exclaims

"Heavens to Mergatroid!"
which is I guess like saying
"Heavens to Betsy!" or "For Pete's Sake."

It might have been Lucy who said it
—I doubt it was Ricky or Fred—
and while we're at it who in heaven's name

are Pete and Betsy? Mergatroid
sounds like the name of a planet
born of an asteroid or the Prime

Minister of such a place. A rock
formation, cousin of kryptonite, enemy
of superguys. Like a superguy, did Mergatroid

inhabit only the realm
of sitcoms and cartoons which are themselves
a kind of hereafter?

Just like Miss Mary Mack-Mack-Mack,
Mergatroid appears to have died out before having
its day in lexicon court. There is

no mention of Mergatroid
in Webster's Ninth or OED,
no clue as to the he, she,

or it of Mergatroid,
the geology, biology,
or pharmacology of Mergatroid.

Perhaps, like those mid-century radio signals
still migrating through the cosmos,
Mergatroid loped quietly off

to heaven, an old mule-god
whose work on Earth was done.
Now, in the blurred esophagus

of outer space, Mergatroid
careens like a capsule pill or spore
waiting to be reabsorbed

in the linguistic gut
of some distant civilization.
Let's hope all language is so resilient

and that somewhere there exists a place
that makes good use of all
we've squandered.

9 Anal Haiku

by Gerry Gomez Pearlberg

why all this scandal?
why such fear of anal glee?
set your anus free!

sunrise in warm fog
like a well-lubed latex glove
pushing the stone gate

cacophony of
plums tumbling from above but
your ass is all I see

in this police state
there are few happy endings
make yours one of them

the grand opening!
just one thing to remember:
don't forget the lube

Orson Welles was a li-
ar. Citizen Kane my ass!
Rosebud was no sled.

because you cannot see it
because it is behind you
you malign the seventh wonder of the world

count your blessings, girl
God gave you a big butt
the more the merrier

sex: a precipice
a sheer, hazardous cliff
but what a great view!

Hurricane and Flood Awareness Month*

by Gerry Gomez Pearlberg

Stubbed Toe Awareness Month
Nuclear War Awareness Month
Toxic Fumes Awareness Month
Nicotine Patch Awareness Month
Lousy Mood Awareness Month
Slippery Floor Awareness Month
Sexual Witchhunt Awareness Month
Unwitting Accomplice Awareness Month
UFO-sized Umbrellas Awareness Month
Too-Much-Bleach-In-The-Laundry
  Awareness Month
Overcooked Pasta Awareness Month
Condescending Waiters Awareness Month
High Speed Chase Awareness Month
Poisonous Mushroom Awareness Month
Spiders Are Our Friends! Awareness Month
Public Urination Awareness Month
Paper Cut Awareness Month
Long Island Accent Awareness Month

---

* In response to the NYC Mayor's Office recently-posted public service announcements proclaiming November "Hurricane and Flood Awareness Month."

Worms on the Pavement Awareness Month

Chemical Warfare Awareness Month

Stroller-Clogged Sidewalks Awareness Month

Whatever-Happened-To-Population-
Control? Awareness Month

Chihuahuas-in-Sweaters Awareness Month

Ingrown Toenail Awareness Month

Not-Enough-Months Awareness Month

Hurricanes-Are-The-Least-Of-Our-Problems
Awareness Month

The-City-Is-Not-An-Easy-Place-to-Live
Awareness Month

Twenty Years and Still...

by Kate Moira Ryan

(*Romaine Brooks sits on a bench in black. Natalie Barney joins her. They are at Gertrude Stein's memorial service.*)

NATALIE: Alice is the most widowed woman I've ever met. What is she going to do with her life now that Gertrude is gone?

ROMAINE: Maybe she'll write another cookbook.

NATALIE: Those recipes. Pretentious recipes. Take a pheasant, take a side of venison, take a freshly caught duck.

ROMAINE: You shoot duck.

NATALIE: She says take a freshly caught duck. Imagine Gertrude out there with a net. The two of them. They give a whole new meaning to the phrase The Well of Loneliness. Twenty years from now no one will remember that cookbook. Or Gertrude's salons where only men and their silent wives were allowed. And that hateful drunk man from Idaho what was his name? Wrote about bulls and the sea. That hateful man who couldn't write a sentence. Twenty years from now no one will remember his name.

ROMAINE: Hemingway.

NATALIE: We didn't allow men in our salon. Not men like that anyway.

ROMAINE: Princess de Polignac. You let her in. She came with her whip and those riding breeches.

NATALIE: We had Mata Hari dancing. Colette holding forth. Dolly Wilde swinging from the chandeliers naked. Now that's a salon, that's a Wednesday afternoon. Remember Gertrude, sending us that book? *The Autobiography of Alice B. Toklas.* Alice and that horrid page boy haircut and that beak. Take a liver of a freshly trapped unicorn wrap it in a coconut frond. Take a breast of a newly slaughtered wombat fry it in virgin coconut oil.

ROMAINE: Janet Flanner said that Gertrude's brother Leo is trying to take away the art. He says the art is his. It isn't hers anymore now that Gertrude's dead.

NATALIE: That art was theirs. Although I don't know why anyone would want to fight over it. What wretched taste she had in art. Picasso. Twenty years from now no one will remember Picasso. Take a freshly bought canary and drown it in brandy. Serve with feathers on. Serve with Beaujolais nouveau. I think Alice goes to a zoo at night and catches the animals.

ROMAINE: I can't believe that after twenty years you still have not gotten over it.

NATALIE: Over what?

ROMAINE: That she called you a dilettante.

NATALIE: She most certainly did not.

ROMAINE: Twenty years and you're still smarting from that remark.

NATALIE: You're mistaken.

ROMAINE: You invited her to your salon and she said that she didn't want to waste her time watching the queen of the dilettantes hold forth.

NATALIE: In twenty years no one will remember who Gertrude Stein was. She'll be dead and forgotten.

ROMAINE: I think it's better to be dead and forgotten then alive and forgotten.

NATALIE: Forgotten? Take the heart of a freshly caught virgin... (*Takes Romaine's hand.*)

ROMAINE: And an incredibly large trust fund.

NATALIE: After all these years.

ROMAINE: I still know how to get you.

NATALIE: Here comes Alice. Hide the dog.

What We Do

by Stephen Cramer

Who knew how percussive
a container the brewers had shaped
till with two feet of pipe
a man beat a keg
so it turned useless
for anything else but to carry

his ungodly rhythms?
The metal contorted to contain
the continuous syncopation
wrecked into its side.
He's drumming a rim full
of dents, angled facets

that pull to themselves
all the sun they can bear
before tossing a tremolo
of light on the bricks behind.
Look around: whatever this sound is
that ricochets the streets

is contagious—less drums
than a seasonal quickening
that everything's so busy
keeping up with, new desire
mixing up the thick torpor
of the past months. At my feet,

two pigeons struggle over
any spare piece of garbage
to entice a female.
They fumble in this patch
of spilled popcorn, gurgling
and churring in figure-eights,

inflating the sheen of their necks
over their turf. Even
when she dodges away,
they just keep flashing
iridescence for no one. Noontime,
the drummer's checking

the metal where he's reflected
in more than one place, tucking
a stray curl behind his ear.
But just so you don't forget
whose block this is,
when a woman goes by

he's sent demonic,
like he knows
this commotion's for keeps,
and he's thrown
into a shimmy of the hips
which he rises out of

just in time to fit
the mechanical stumble
of a far off jackhammer
into his running rhythm,
these sounds the music wants
to encompass, make its own,

so, in the end, you can't tell
if he's playing the drums
or if they're playing him.
'Cause when you're itching
to finish with your wrists
the rumble that begins in your gut,

this is what you do—you're ready
to bang on anything for love.
You'll break your hands
to get that rhythm out.

How I Got to Watch Whitey Ford Win His 24th Game

by Janice Levy

I HID BEHIND THE LIVING ROOM COUCH AND PEEKED out the window. My brothers were at it again. Moe scratched his poison ivy and wiped his hands on Larry's cheeks. Larry bit baby Satan's foot. Satan spit up sweet potatoes over the alligator logo on my dad's tennis shirt.

My mother bent her head toward her pregnant stomach and whispered. She thought a baby would repeat what it heard in the womb. She was sure this one's first word would start with an "f."

"Get in the car. Everyone. Now." My father swept them down the front path, his arms like windmills. The vein on his forehead pulsed like a green worm. He moaned at his watch. We had a plane to catch. Our summer vacation had begun.

"Snake!" Moe hissed, spraying the garden hose. Larry bumped into my mother, who fell into a rose bush, propelling Satan through the air into my father's arms for a touchdown.

"I hate vacations," my mom said, her voice as prickly as the thorns she pulled from her skin. "I'm not having fun."

"Not fun. Not fun." Moe and Larry stomped their feet. They stacked up our three suitcases, put Satan on top and moved back for a flying leap. My dad's hand turned into a lobster claw as he grabbed my brothers by the neck. Satan added peas to my father's tennis shirt.

"Morris! Lawrence! And where's Carlee?"

My dad's face was gray and puffy like a rain-cloud. He dragged the suitcases to the curb, took a deep breath and blew everyone into the car.

As he opened the trunk, I yelled out,"The Yankees are winning, top of the first, nobody out." I waved from the window. I was still in my pajamas.

My father slammed the trunk shut, spun around and leaped like a grasshopper. He scooped me up in his arms.

"Dad," I said. "You forgot–"

"Not another word, Curly," he said. "Zip it."

My brothers and I wrestled in the back seat. We crushed pretzel logs. We stuck cheese doodles up our nose. "I might as well be driving a bunch of hogs to market," my dad said. We squealed and oinked. My mom covered her stomach and sang opera scales.

"Why are we leaving an air-conditioned house to squeeze into a two room shack with holes in the screens—"my mom said.

"—and mattresses like mashed potatoes," Moe said.

"—and a swamp for a lake," said Larry.

"—and there's no T.V. to watch the Yankees," I said.

"The Yankees?" My dad hit the brake.

"Whitey Ford is pitching and—"

"Zip it Curly," he said. "Or I will."

My father drove down the block, cursing the traffic, the weather, cheese doodles and Whitey Ford. He threw in a few combinations towards my mom's stomach.

"Who left the gas tank empty?" he said. We all pointed to Satan.

We stopped at Albert's Gas Station. "Where's my wallet?" my dad asked. He patted his pockets as if he had fleas. "Who took my wallet?"

We all pointed to Satan. My dad slapped his forehead. "I left my wallet on top of the luggage when I went to pack the car," he said. He opened the trunk then slammed it down so hard the car shook.

"Where's the luggage?" My dad's voice sounded like his underwear had been pulled up around his ears. "Who took the luggage?" We all pointed to Satan.

"You left the suitcases at the curb," I said.

"Why didn't you—"

I zipped up my lips.

The gas station attendant, Albert, squinted at my father. "Cash," he said.

"Listen," my dad said. "I've got a plane to catch. Can't we work this out?"

Albert spit, nicking my father's sneaker.

"O.K., I'll be right back. I'll get my wallet. You can have my wife. I'll leave her with you until I come back."

My mom said she wasn't staying unless there was a decent place to sit down because grease stains didn't come out and that she hoped Albert's teeth fell out from all that chewing tobacco.

"Maybe we can work this out another way," Albert yelled, as our car pulled away.

"Satan stinks!" I said, as my dad dropped him in my lap. My father's jaw jutted like an iron.

My dad went faster, the car shaking like a bucking stallion. We leaned out the windows and screamed like moose. Moe threw Satan's diaper in the front seat. Larry asked if we were going to get a new mother and suggested 'Lolita' from the magazines my dad hid in the garage. My father cursed all of my mom's relatives, even the ones who had died. I wondered if Albert liked opera.

My father drove through a red light. Satan revved his voice like a siren, louder and louder, until a real one drowned him out.

The policeman cracked his knuckles. "You passed a red light, crossed a double yellow line and I clocked you at going 80. Who started the fire?"

We all pointed to Satan.

Moe wanted to touch his gun. Larry asked how many people he had killed.

"Today?" The cop said and stared at my pajamas. "License and registration," he said to my dad.

My dad gulped like a bull frog. "We've got a plane to catch, Officer and—"

"He made my mom pregnant, then left her with Albert," Moe said.

"Then he kidnapped me," Larry said.

"I was watching the Yankees," I said.

"The Yankees?" The policeman frowned at my dad and scribbled on his pad. "While Whitey Ford was pitching?"

"Officer," my dad puckered his lips like a fish. "I left my license in my wallet, which is on top of the luggage that I left at the curb of my house unless somebody stole—"

"Or put back in the house because I left the door open," I said.

"You left the door open?" My father's eye twitched.

"Well, you left Mom at the gas station," I said.

"She's going to have a baby," Moe said.

"And it's going to say the 'f' word," Larry said.

Satan wailed. His cheeks looked like soggy tomatoes. The policeman held his nose. "Who's this?" he asked.

"Shemp," my father said.

"Shemp?!" We all said. Satan stopped crying for the first time in six months. Then threw up on my father's neck.

The policeman rubbed his chin as if trying to change its shape. He added numbers on three pages. "Your inspection sticker is overdue. One brake light is out."

My father clasped his wrists together and sighed. "Officer, arrest me. Just take me away."

Which he did.

The police station had a small T.V. set. And that's how I got to watch Whitey Ford win his twenty-fourth game.

Kleptomania

by Wayne Koestenbaum

Find a useful Latin phrase
to describe the escapist sunburst color of the barge
arriving at my doorstep,
a "come all ye faithful" iridescence.

*

Don't use the voice and it will last forever.
Maybe one day we'll rent a Greek villa and read biographies
on the beach together!
Then, perhaps, I'll turn my back on truth.

*

Milton Berle caught me stealing his best line.
I returned it.
Milton's wife should have known better
than to serve me kippers for lunch.

*

Much happens on Sixth Avenue.
If only my Bugs Bunny complex would calm down,
then I could outfox Duchamp at Bonnard's game,
despite what the historians say.

The Visible

by Wayne Koestenbaum

1.

"From a distance
it is perfectly visible,"

she said of her vagina.
"God put it rather high."

It's not her fault
she has no taste.

2.

Drugged, she took a bus
to visit me: how loyal.

She cooked me an omelette,
mocked my former meals:

"Your idea of dinner
was cold cuts!"

3.

Her son died.
Her son was sexy.

Her son had a wife.
Her son had a built-in pool.

I sat by the son's poolside.
I touched the son in the dark.

From a distance
he was perfectly visible.

Spa Moods

by Wayne Koestenbaum

1.

A spa mood hits. I duck.
It goes away.

I sit up.
It hits again.

Why not swing
wide the door?

2.

A pinhead
whose ontology

needs burping,
I lean on

this instant's
impromptu

scaffolding—
and it falls.

3.
I wish I could claim
victory, but I hate

to organize
steam clouds.

4.

Eclectic pastoral:
I'm wearing

too much makeup,
or not enough.

I miss confetti,
lacunae.

I'm on a premonition
streak, don't stop me.

Dark and Luscious

from the forthcoming novel *The Amity Warriors*

by Carolyn Ferrell

WHAT REMAINED THE SAME YEAR AFTER YEAR WAS the *hair* talk; you talked and talked and wound up nowhere—it was the same thing as being in a desert in Africa with only a bicycle to get you around. Sunshine Drug always had a tiny rack in back for shampoos and straightening combs and pomades; by the time I got to high school and was taking care of my mother fresh from cancer at the Good Samaritan Hospital, the rack in Sunshine Drug had been replaced by a full shelf, and then a few years later by an entire aisle up in the front of the store marked *Ethnic*. There were so many things to buy, your fingers hurt with imagination. My mother's head by then was bald as a cucumber, but she insisted on a hairnet, a package full of blond bobby pins, and Queen Nefertiti Hair Spray. I noticed these things alongside the others as I went there to purchase cotton balls, moisturizers, herbal hair conditioners, pain relievers, Epsom Salts, and eventually loads and loads of prescriptions for my mother, all designed to keep her life raging against the oblivious currents of a death away from home.

There was good hair and bad hair, and on North Moss Drive, the fence was over-loaded to the one side. You counted Crystal Rogers and Punch Bean, who were *Already Women*, and then there were the rest of the girls whose hair was not like a mink coat. *Burnt, nappy, charcoal, toasted, roasted, African, jungle, c.p., country, ugly as sin:* we heard the words come out our mouths as we stood waiting for the bus in the morning. Some girls liked to say they were dark and luscious, but they could not bring themselves to believe it. Because of my mother I did not count; my hair was called *cheating* by most of North Moss Drive.

I inherited my MAMA'S GOOD HAIR, Mrs. Effie Washington told my mother over the clothesline one morning last year. She was astronomical, wearing her hair in two flippy strands of dusty brown string that was supposedly called a *hairdo.* My mother hunched over the laundry basket. This was before she got sick in the breast over by the ferris wheel; looking in her shirt at the top of the ride, feeling a knobby nut pinching at her new bra underwire. This was before then. She listened to Effie.

I think her grandfather or great grandfather was a Dutchman, Mrs. Washington said. *Coming from the land of windmills. Do you know, Mrs. Clark, that they are credited with discovering many parts of this world?* The plastic clothes pins were clumped together in Mrs. Washington's mouth like willing victims.

I can't do anything with this mop, my mother sighed, tapping her head with a wooden clothespin. *I wish I had hair like my daughters. They have good hair.*

Mrs. Effie Washington stopped hanging her husband's shirts on the line and looked over at me, lying on top of the laundry basket in the grass, wearing just my bathing suit, and no shorts to cover up my butt or the waves of flesh on my chicken thighs. She said, *Her hair's cheating, Mrs. Clark.* Then, staring at her shirts on the line, she added, *You got to count your blessings that, though, that the girl has brains.*

*

If you talked *hair* like a regular girl on North Moss Drive, or like Peaches Mountain, my best friend Mozelle's brother who wanted to *be a* girl, then you stood with your right hand on your right hip on the front steps to your house and with your left hand you blew kisses to people of all persuasions or maybe you curled a wisp of reddish-brownish-blackish hair, flattened by your mother's hot curlers or shattered by the relaxer that the boy who worshiped your lips; *Apply Generously and Often;* and then on the steps you contemplated the unfair twists and turns of life that had been dealt you, so you shouted out to the *other* girls, the ones who made fun of you, the ones who stood around the boys parked in broken-down cars and inhaled their cigarette smoke for them, you with a *sassified* self that could knock down the walls of any swollen-headed church on Long Island and any of its stupefied inhabitants, you shouted, *Looks like someone got them burn marks on the back of their neck again, don't it? Miss Lynette Snaggle-Tooth-a-Liscious?*

If you said those kinds of things with those kind of *Mannish Guts*, you never got smacked; you never had to wait in the school cafeteria to get your butt beat after hot lunch; you never had a multi-color ballpoint pen write all over the back of your shirt while you took a social studies test on the Pharaohs of ancient Egypt: Freak. Freak. You also did not have a mismatch family at home, like mine, or a mother who bent over way too much these days, or a relentless girl named Punch Beane for a new best friend who kept telling you not to worry because we were all Woman Comrades in the Skin and that over our Dead Bodies would we see the end of *Whitey* together. Plus no fags in the Revolution. *Just get that Peaches Mountain out your head. And Concentrate.*

*

Whitey was my mother. That was no secret. Her hair floated in chocolate-blond strands over the front of her face as she picked out her favorite tomato from the Association Supermarket. She cornered the clerk and asked why the buttermilk still had not come in. In my mother's heart she missed the country she'd been born in, but would not go back there if you paid her a million bucks. Her breasts became sick, but that did not stop the river of love. She had reams and reams of tenderness for everyone on North Moss Drive when you thought about it: if only they had stopped calling her names, if only they'd learned to read her like a book. She was not the opposite of love.

My mother knew things, but preferred to keep it all on the Q.T. She watched Walter Cronkite and folded the clothes from the laundry basket. When we asked her questions about this and that, though, she became sandwiched in anger: No, she would not go back to Germany, no she would not divorce our father. No she was not going to die. This is just a routine check-up for gray spots on the x-ray.

No she did not hate the Black Race. She loved the Black Race. *Just why, though, do they have to be in the War? They have absolutely nothing to gain,* was her mind.

Then she'd say to us, *I can't believe you'd ask that junk,* as she mated green sock with green sock, halter top with hot pants, folding each towel as if it were her own child. Later, in the backyard with the sun steaming down, she would prune the geraniums around the edge of the patio and snarl, *If one of those bastards writes Pig on our garage door again, I'll take them out in cold blood.*

If you lived on North Moss Drive and were NORMAL, then you just went to school and came home and watched *I Spy* and lived a perfect life. Your new best friend was not in her twenties but in a state of Arrested Development. Your old best friend like you in the Sixth Grade was not afraid of you together with your new best friend. You did not love a boy whose hair stood like a tower of marshmallows like the Bride of Frankenstein. You did not think your mother was going to die in her sleep, leaving you to catch a wisp of her hair as she breezed into heaven.

If you lived on North Moss Drive and were normal, your hair was as tightly curled and as bergamot-scented and normal as the crystal chandelier hanging in your family's dining room.

From the second grade on: the mothers of the girls on North Moss Drive liked to put their hands on my head when they saw me at the Association Supermarket and rub it like I was Aladdin. *If only my girl could do her hair like this*, they would fantasize, only there wasn't anything particular about my hair except for it was in two braids and it was straight. The STRAIGHT was what I saw in their eyes, though.

You got your mama's hair, was what I heard whispered by their daughters, standing at the bus stop, waiting year in and out, tightly-headed, turning into young women in sun and wind. There was a grazing in their eyes as they looked me over, one full of mornings and evenings at the kitchen table or in the dining room under a mother's warm brown hands and comb. You might turn out looking like Angela Davis or if you were lucky, that lady from the Fifth Dimension. *You got your mama's hair.* We did not have a chandelier in our dining room because my father did not believe my mother was that sick; besides, he had other ideas about lifting my family up from these so-called petty people on North Moss Drive. We did not know whether he liked the Black

Race because he put nothing in his hair, no Afro-Sheen, no oils or liquids; the flakes just flew. *We're not made of money*, was his favorite saying; he also did not care too much for that favorite tomato, imported from Holland. Too expensive.

We never owned a chandelier, even though my mother always wished we did. *It would make me feel a whole lot better*, she told him, but his ears could not see. Then my mother said she was tired of feeling like a pauper when she went over to the Hutchinsons' and Lord knows they did not have a lot of cash, look at those rags they have on their heads; and just as you pass those god-awful slip covers in the parlor, there was their *diamond* chandelier from White's Department Store just staring her in the face. It was much too much for any woman, sick or no, to take.

Why do we need a chandelier? My father asked, tearing the newspaper into shreds right before our eyes. We would never be that petty, *ever*, he said, especially to my mother.

I secretly wished for a chandelier, a *real sparkler*, one I could hang a Black Power Flag from, like the flag Punch Bean had hanging over the mirror in her bedroom. Her parents did not allow that thing into the dining room, or anywhere near their chandelier. She was not allowed to get high: They told her to stop acting so street—did they raise her like that? They told her to take that Afro Pik out her hair and start behaving like a decent young lady. Go to church, find herself a decent man. *Your father and me, we seen things. We sat at lunch counters and had our heads bashed in.* Then they shoveled the candied yams onto her plate.

On the school bus, James Brown reached over and squeezed my thighs like loaves of Butter Top bread. *You got your mama's hair,* he whispered to me, on the way to Park Avenue, his eyes lolling back into his head for miles and miles; when I looked at him tiny oval face, I saw what he would look like *as a man.* I was sure the bus driver could see this hand mull over me, but she was too tired to say anything except yell at us to stick our heads back into the bus. She would wind through the tunnel underneath the Long Island Home which was a *Psychiatric Hospital* to get her point across, a short cut to the Junior High, and fear would reach even a person like James Brown, who was mortified of the dark.

On the way home, I jumped out of the bus and ran to my house crying, careful not to let the others see me, careful to be like the wind in their presence; *my mama's hair, my mama's hair, no, you mean my* MOTHER'S *hair*; and in the corner of my escape was Peaches, standing on the front steps to his house, right hand on right hip, smiling, searching me with his eyes—he had been thrown out of school for *unmanly activities* and, according to Harriet-Ann Hutchinson, was not supposed to return to Amity Junior High until he started liking girls again; til then, he was supposed to go the Hollywood Baptist School to complete the Eighth Grade. And there was also that boy who said he could relax hair like he was the Hair Queen of the world; he was in the same class as Peaches and the other boys and girls struggling in subjects like Geometry and the ancient Pharaohs and God's meaning in our life. There was that boy and there was Peaches.

He watched me run from the school bus. He did not know I had a crush on him that was as *stupefying* as an ocean. I did not care what they said—I would marry him and do his hair for him every single day. *His hair ignited my soul*. It made my insides burn in a way that made the universe forgettable. All I had to do was see him on the front steps; or listen to Mozelle tell me how much she loved my mother and wished hers was sick like mine too, maybe she would treat her and Peaches better; or watch Peaches as he sat in front of their mother's mirror at 52 North Moss Drive, fingering the feather necklaces she'd hung there, whispering old songs to himself. He would try with no luck to pull his fingers through his hair. He would wish his hair went some other way, so he too could be loved on the block.

As I left the school bus that day, I zoomed home worse than if my life depended on it. Peaches watched from his yard as I floated up to my front steps and began squeezing the screen door handle like a maniac. I did not want him to see me that way, frightened, afraid of my hair and the way it sang out to others, but it was too late. Inside my house, my mother would be sitting at the sewing machine, trying to pump out two more dresses for me and my sister before she had to go back to the hospital. Her foot would be turning and turning. She would be thinking of a time before children, when her breasts had no worries at all.

I looked back, about to blow him a kiss, but then of course he was magically transported—standing thousands and thousands of miles in the distance of the sky, his head wrapped up in an indigo scarf. Peaches had clouds in his voice.

This was the boy I loved. He liked to blow kisses. He could learn to love me. I could have believed anything in the universe right then if you asked me; I could even have ridden a bike through the blazing sands of the desert. Even though, as I stood there, Peaches' face faded behind a gauze of incense and hymn books, and his hair draped the ground in an infinite rainbow. There truly was a Heaven, and it was staring me in the face.

I blew him a sugar-soaked kiss. In real life, however, Peaches shouted back to me, *Just where do you think you can run to, Sarah, you hair-brained child?*

Because He Liked to Look at It

from the play *The Vagina Monologues*

by Eve Ensler

THIS IS HOW I CAME TO LOVE MY VAGINA. IT'S EMbarrassing because it's not politically correct. I mean I know it should have happened in a bath with salt grains from the Dead Sea, Enya playing, me loving my woman self. I know the story. Vaginas are beautiful. Our self-hatred is only the internalized repression and hatred of the patriarchal culture. It isn't real. Pussies Unite. I know all of it. Like if we'd grown up in a culture where we were taught fat thighs were beautiful, we'd all be pounding down milkshakes and cookies, lying on our backs, spending our days thigh expanding. But, we didn't grow up in that culture. I hated my thighs and I hated my vagina even more. I thought it was incredibly ugly. I was one of those women who had looked at it and from that moment on I wished I hadn't. It made me sick. I pitied anyone who had to go down there.

In order to survive, I began to pretend there was something else between my legs. I imagined furniture—cozy futons with light cotton comforters, little velvet settees, leopard rugs, or pretty things—silk handkerchiefs, quilted pot holders, or place settings or miniature landscapes—clear crystal lakes, or moisty Irish bogs. I got so accustomed to this that I lost all memory of having a vagina. Whenever a man was inside me, I pictured him inside a mink-lined muffler, or a red rose, or a Chinese bowl.

Then I met Bob. Bob was the most ordinary man I ever met. He was thin and tall and nondescript and wore khaki tan clothes. Bob did not like spicy foods or listen to Prodigy. He had no interest in sexy lingerie. In the summer he spent time in the shade. He did not share his inner feelings. He did not have any problems or issues and was not even an alcoholic. He wasn't very funny or articulate or mysterious. He wasn't mean or unavailable. He wasn't self-involved or charismatic. He didn't drive fast. To be honest, I didn't particularly like Bob. I would have missed him altogether if he hadn't picked up my change that I dropped on the deli floor. When he handed me back my quarters and pennies and his hand accidentally touched mine, something happened. I went to bed with him. That's when the miracle occurred.

Turned out that Bob loved vaginas. He was a connoisseur. He loved the way they felt, the way they tasted, the way they smelled, but most importantly he loved the way they looked. He had to look at them. The first time we had sex, he told me he had to see me.

"I'm right here," I said.

"No, you," he said. "I have to see you."

"Turn on the light," I said, thinking he was a weirdo and freaking out in the dark. He turned on the light.

Then he said, "O.K., I'm ready, ready to see you."

"Right here," I waved. "I'm right here."

He began to undress me.

"What are you doing, Bob?" I said.

"I need to see you," he replied.

"No need," I said. "Just do it."

"I need to see what you look like," he said.

"But you've seen a red leather couch before," I said. "You've seen a sunflower. You've seen a Chinese bowl. I'm sure you've seen that."

Bob continued. He would not stop. I wanted to throw up and die.

"This is awfully intimate," I said. "Can't you just do it?"

"No," he said. "It's who you are. I need to look."

I held my breath. He looked and looked. He gasped and smiled and stared and groaned. He got breathy and his face changed. He didn't look ordinary anymore. He looked like a hungry beautiful beast.

"You're so beautiful," he said. "You're elegant and deep and innocent and wild."

"You saw that there?" I said.

It was like he read my palm.

"I saw that," he said, "and more, much much more."

He stayed looking for almost an hour as if he were studying a map, observing the moon, staring into my eyes, but it was my vagina. In the light I watched him looking at me and he was so genuinely excited, so peaceful and euphoric, I began to get wet and turned on. I began to see myself the way he saw me. I began to feel beautiful and delicious—like a great painting, or a waterfall. Bob wasn't afraid. He wasn't grossed out. I began to swell, began to feel proud. Began to love my vagina. And Bob, lost himself there and I was there with him, in my vagina, and we were gone.

Humor Is Revolutionary

A Conversation with Eve Ensler

by Susan Thomsen
edited by Betsey Osborne

Eve Ensler's plays include Floating Rhoda and The Glue Man *(published in The Best Plays of 1993), the acclaimed* Extraordinary Measures, The Depot *(directed by Joanne Woodward),* Scooncat, Loud in My Head, Lemonade, Ladies, Reef and Particle, *and* Cinderella Cendrillion *(directed by Anne Bogart).*

Her play The Vagina Monologues *won a 1997 Obie Award and was nominated for a Drama Desk Award and recently a Helen Hayes Award. Currently enjoying a run Off Broadway, it has toured America and the world, playing in sold-out houses in Oklahoma City, Baltimore, Atlanta, Dallas, Seattle, and Washington, D.C., as well as Jerusalem, Berlin, Zagreb, and London. It was the centerpiece for V-Day, a gala theatrical and musical event featuring artists and guests including Whoopi Goldberg, Winona Ryder, Glenn Close, and Susan Sarandon, on Valentine's Day, 1998, at the Hammerstein Ballroom, in New York. V-Day raised consciousness and funds to stop violence against women. A second V-Day event was held in London at the Old Vic in February, 1999, featuring Cate Blanchett, Kate Winslet, Melanie Griffith, and Gillian Anderson, among others.* The Vagina Monologues, *now a best-seller, was published by Villard in February, 1998.*

Eve's play Necessary Targets, *commissioned by the Joseph Papp Public Theater, was given a performance on Broadway, starring Meryl Streep, Angelica Houston, and Cherry Jones, to benefit Bosnian women refugees. It was also performed at the National Theater in Sarajevo with Glenn Close, Marisa Tomei, and a cast of Bosnian actors, and was performed this winter in honor of First Lady Hillary Rodham Clinton at the Kennedy Center for the Performing Arts.*

Eve Ensler is working on a new play, Conviction, *and a screenplay,* Seven Counts. *Her next book,* Points of Reentry, *which explores women's relationships with their bodies, will be published by Villard in February, 2001.*

EVE ENSLER AND I MET FOR BREAKFAST AT A MANhattan restaurant on the morning that the Senate impeachment trial began last January. Eve was just back from Washington where she had performed an extended, acclaimed run of *The Vagina Monologues* at the Studio Theatre; I had recently seen the play there. She was about to head off to London to present the show at the King's Head, Islington, and to inaugurate the first British V-Day fundraiser. I was so absorbed in our conversation and so interested in what she had to say that, until I listened to my tape later, I had no idea how loud our surroundings—sputtering cappuccino machines, chatty fellow diners—were. Meeting Eve was like meeting an old friend I hadn't seen for a long time and catching up. And that's what she imparts from the stage: an accessible immediacy that captures your attention and lets you laugh, cry and, most of all, lets you think. The following is an excerpt from our talk.

SUSAN THOMSEN: I got this tape recorder recently, and I think it's a concert recorder where you hold it up. So if I go to a Phish concert, I'll be all set.

EVE ENSLER (*to waiter*): Could I get a little foam?

ST: Were you an actor as a kid?

EE: No.

ST: No?

EE: No. I acted a little in college, but no. I love the idea of creating characters. I love the idea of creating people, of inhabiting people, of becoming other people, because I've always loved people so much. And when I was a kid, in order to escape my own reality, which I was constantly trying to do, I would enter other people's realities. I would pretend I was them. I would live in them. So, it was a setup for later on becoming a playwright.

ST: Playwriting to me is a little added act of generosity. There's both the writing and something else that makes it so immediate for the audience.

EE: Well, I actually began as a poet. And then I loved theater, and I started to direct. So, it was as though poetry and directing merged into playwriting. The theater is an incredibly sacred place. When the lights go down, you have a captive audience that is willing to sit there. It's a place where there is community, where people gather together in community. Also I've always lived in a more dramatic zone. When I was younger, people called me Sarah Bernhardt. What's normal for me is seen as dramatic, heightened reality.

[*Waiter approaches.*]

ST: Do you want to get something to eat?

EE: Could I get some scrambled egg whites?

WAITER: Sure. With whole wheat or white toast?

EE: No...Do you have any little potatoes? What kind of potatoes do you have?

WAITER: Home fried.

EE: Yeah, perfect. You're not going to get anything?

ST: I'll probably get something to go later.

ST: Well, you seem to like accents, too. You do them really well in your show.

EE: How we come to know people is by becoming them. And that's what theater allows us to do; it's a heightened form of compassion.

ST: I think you're right.

ST: What's the relationship between your performance and your playwriting? You're not always in your plays, right?

EE: This [*The Vagina Monologues*] is the only time I've ever been in one.

ST: The only time?

EE: Well, I did write one other piece during the Iraq War called *Dicks in the Desert*, which was a protest against the first Iraqi bombing. I performed it because I needed a channel for the incredible despair and outrage I was feeling. But performing *The Vagina Monologues* was accidental. Secretly I had always wanted to do it, but I never owned it. It was buried in there someplace. But when I finished writing it, I felt so connected to the women I'd interviewed that I didn't want to turn it into a "play," and give it to actors. I wanted to tell these women's stories so I could stay with them. It began casually. I was telling their stories in little downtown clubs and stuff, and then it grew to be this other thing.

ST: Where was the first place you performed *The Vagina Monologues*?

EE: At the Westside Arts Theatre. There was this little festival and I did a few monologues from it. That was the very first time. And every time I did it, people would say ah, this is great, this is something new and I'd have no idea if that were true or not. And then I had another show running in New York at Here, where they said to me, Why don't you do three nights of *The Vagina Monologues*? And I did, and Alexis Greene, a critic, ended up writing, unbeknownst to me, a wonderful review [in *Theater-Week*]. I felt encouraged by it, which may be the only time. Even when reviews are good, you rarely feel encouraged by them because they so rarely get what you're doing.

ST: It seems like *The Vagina Monologues* is something people, especially women, are anxious to hear. I saw a lot of big groups of friends in Washington. I can see why people would come up to you and tell you stories afterwards because you really are talking to the audience directly.

EE: The idea of the piece was to make it very personal and very specific and in the present tense so people could feel that they were included in the whole process. Lots of people come and tell me their stories and write me and, you know, feel like they're a part of it—which they are!

ST: What is the relationship between your politics and your connections with women and the work that you do?

EE: A few years ago I made a decision that I was going to commit my life on a political level to ending violence towards women. It sums everything else up: If violence towards women were to end, the world would substantially change. The empowerment of women and the healing of women and the representation of women—anything that involves women—have been what interested me. It's not that I'm uninterested in men, but I feel like men have already been talked about. They've been—They're everywhere. They exist in the culture. I don't think we're represented fully anywhere.

ST: Right. Men have been used as the measuring stick, the standard.

EE: Exactly. They exist. It's their world. And I've always been interested in what's invisible.

ST: Tell me about V-Day and doing it at the colleges.

EE: When I started performing around the world, so many women would come up to me to talk about how they've been violated. It began to be devastating to my psyche—having this much information and not doing anything about it. Night after night to hear about battery and rape and genital mutilation and incest was unbelievable. I'm a Buddhist and I was chanting on a regular basis to see what my mission is here, to be clear about purpose. And one day I was chanting and it suddenly got clear: stop violence towards women. That's what you're doing here. That's it. So, I started to think how could I really serve that notion. And in a big way. Not in a little way. Not in an embarrassed, please-give-me-permission, I'm-apologetic kind of way but in a we're-seriously-going-to-do-something-to-stop-violence way. And V-Day emerged. Start a day, or a movement, to end violence towards women and call it V-Day and have Valentine's Day be that day, which is in theory the day of love and romance? Take the romance out of Valentine's Day and put the vagina back in. So last year [1998] we initiated V-Day.

I do believe that in these next few years women are going to come into their power. I know it in my body. I can feel it. And the response to V-Day was enormous. It was easy to do in a way. Because whether they were actors or whether they were coming to the theater or whether they were working on the event, people were fully there. And the event kept getting bigger and bigger and bigger, to the point where we did it in 2500-seat theater. We sold all those tickets for a hundred dollars and more and raised a lot of money to stop violence towards women. And that became this kind of fuel, indicating, "Yes, a movement is possible. Let's go."

ST: That's great.

EE: V-Day is spreading. This V-Day, I'm so excited because 61 colleges have already signed up. Arizona State University has bands, they have an art show, they have 23 women performing the piece, and they're printing T-shirts. And all the money at all these colleges is going to local groups that work to stop violence. And then we're going to be doing V-Day at the Old Vic this year in London. Same thing we did last year, with English and American stars. And then it's going to be done all over the world on that day. So we hope that by the year 2001, it's going to be the big event at Madison Square Garden. I'm writing a new piece. By then we will have spawned a huge movement.

ST: I totally believe it's possible.

EE: Something big is happening, and as I travel around the

world with the piece, I see how much women want. We formed a coalition over in London, and 50 to 70 women are showing up for every meeting to organize this event. It's a big deal, and it's because every woman I know has had it. It's, like, over.

ST: And here we are on the day that the Senate impeachment trial starts. They don't seem to have a plan. I can barely think about it. It makes me weep.

EE: Me, too. It makes me so sad. But it's the collapse of male reality. I think we've gone as far with that as we can go. I do. It's over. It's like in *As I Lay Dying* when the body is still in the house at the beginning of the novel and everybody sits there with it. That's kind of how I feel about male reality. Let's get the corpse out of the house, and start going. The stink is absorbing all our attention.

ST: Can you tell us about some of your other projects?

EE: I have a play about Bosnia, *Necessary Targets*, and we're performing it for Hillary Clinton next week, at the Kennedy Center. V-Day is presenting it because the play is about stopping violence towards women. And I'm writing a comedy about Prozac.

ST: Is that *Oklahoma: Not the Musical*?

EE: No, that's something else. The Prozac thing I shouldn't be writing because I have all these commissions, but, of course, being a person who defies authority at all costs, I am. I'm working on that and then on a new play for the Music-Theater Group, which is based on the life of a political revolutionary. It's a play about sisters; it's called *Conviction*. It should be finished in the spring. And then I have the new book, which Villard is publishing, called *Points of Reentry: Tits, Ass, Cunts, Thighs, and Teeth*. That's going to be the performance text for V-Day 2001. I'm interviewing women all over the world about the parts of their bodies that they systematically hate, destroy, mutilate, hide in order to fit in with their particular culture. Just to see how much energy women spend hating some aspect of their body. Our whole lives there's a focus there. So, rather than running countries, we're hating our thighs or expanding our breasts or shrinking our butts. I'm interviewing women all over the world. So, it will be kind of a global piece about the body. *Oklahoma: Not the Musical* I probably won't start until next summer. I'm doing a whole, big piece about the bombing. Then I just finished this film called *Seven Counts* for Glenn Close. I spent a year in a prison interviewing women. It's a film based on four women's stories.

ST: When does that come out, do you know?

EE: I just finished the draft, so now we're waiting to hear about production.

ST: Eve, how do you find the time?

EE: I don't know.

ST: I read what you're doing and I feel like I have to lie down and rest.

EE: You? I think I'm going to drop dead. It's the performance thing that has been hard.

ST: It must be so draining.

EE: I used to be intense about writing. I wrote all the time, but now, between writing and performing and being an activist and then trying to have a life, it's been intense. But it's great. I'm not complaining. After I get done with *Oklahoma*—I'm telling myself this—and the book, I'm going to take a break—until I get another idea! What happens when you get supported and when you get some success, you get a lot more energy. Or I do. It generates more ideas and then I go, "Oh, I could do this or do that."

ST: Do you think that the desire to put yourself out there makes you keep doing it, too?

EE: There are a couple of things. Ending violence towards women is a big motor in my work. We only live so long; I only have so much time to work on this issue. I want to be able to know that I did as much as I could while I was alive to end violence towards women. So, that's my motor. Then there's the artistic motor, that I only have so much time to write. I want to be able to do as much as possible. I love writing. I love working. People say, "You're a workaholic," and I say, "Well, what else are we doing here?" I don't get what people do besides work. You go to the beach? What is that? I don't see work as pain. I love work.

ST: It does seem to me that for people who have a lot of success with their work, it's an integrated part of their life.

EE: It's their life—and unapologetically so. I feel like it's taken me years to get to the point where people are finally coming to see my work. Paying me to do my work. I'm so excited that this has occurred. Why wouldn't I be working all the time? It's kind of like, okay, now finally I can do my work.

ST: Would you talk a little bit about your evolution as an artist?

EE: When I was younger, I had passion and a lot of motivation, but structurally I had no idea what I was doing. I just didn't know as much. You lack wisdom; you lack layers of understanding of texture when you're younger. As a playwright, my work didn't have much resonance. Not that it was terrible, but the greatest thing about being a writer is that if you keep writing you get better. And you begin to come into your voice. Before, you jam against it, trying, and it's awkward, and one day you go, "Oh, this is me. This is my voice." It's stripping away all pretensions, in order to tell the truth. So, my evolution emotionally has been coming out of a real, painful life, where I was very abused and very damaged and very broken and very much a victim—and very much seeing myself as a victim. The biggest switch in my life is not doing that any more, by taking back my life. That gives enormous creative energy. And it got me out of black and white, yes and no, polarized thinking: good/bad people, evil people/good people. I don't think that way any more.

ST: Well, how did you take back your life?

EE: Partly through politics and being an activist, and through service. Serving homeless women or serving communities in need. But a major factor for me was doing *The Vagina Monologues*, performing it. Intellectually I had taken back my life a long time ago. It wasn't until it went into the body that things changed. I think theater is the place of the body. I think theater can be the theater of the body. Until it gets to people on that level—and there are so many feminists who are in horrible, self-mutilating relationships. Intellectually they know what's right, but in their body they can't change it—for women until it gets to your cunt, until it gets to the vital part of your sexual motor, it doesn't mean very much...because you keep repeating the same patterns. So, the biggest change for me in my life was doing this piece. There's no doubt about it. My level of confidence—living in my sexuality without fear or apology—that's what's really changed.

ST: Your work is painful in many ways and yet wildly funny. Can you talk a little bit about that?

EE: If all I do for the rest of my life is make people laugh I'll be really happy because I love writing funny stuff. And I love to laugh. I don't love anything more than to laugh. But so few things make me laugh. *The Vagina Monologues* has become like standup.

ST: Oh, in D.C., people in the audience were crying they were laughing so hard.

EE: When I was younger I was scared to do it. I wanted everyone to see the light, and I had my politics. Then I worked with Joanne Woodward. She directed my play *The Depot*. And after the first draft she said to me, "I want it funny." And I thought, "Funny? I'm writing a play about nuclear war. How am I going to make this funny?" She and Shirley Knight taught me about humor. They taught me the funnier, the better. Something begins to happen when you're laughing that can't happen any other time. So try to make the bombing in Oklahoma funny. But you know what? That's the job. How do you take something that's devastating, awful and make it funny? Then people can hear it.

ST: For the *Oklahoma* play, are you interviewing people and using a similar process to the one you used in *The Vagina Monologues*?

EE: Yeah, I'm interviewing all kinds of people. What I'm probably going to end up doing is six different versions of the story. Six different takes on what happened there. I performed in Oklahoma City and was shocked. Over 200 buildings were taken down. I'm interested in the militia. When I was younger I was very didactic and narrow in my thinking. There were good people and bad people, and right people and wrong people. I had no space for tolerance. Now I'm interested in why people are doing what they're doing. Not that I don't have politics with respect to them, I certainly do, but I'm more interested in how we're going to change things as opposed to being right. When I was younger, it was more about "Aren't I great and aren't I right—and I have the whole perspective and you're wrong." When you get older, you see the world in a different way. *The Vagina Monologues* is much less didactic than other things I've written and less polarizing. It's full of duality. I don't know that it's always politically correct, but at the core, there's a real solid message.

ST: Oh, definitely. It seems to me that part of the message is love.

EE: Yes. It's a big part of the message.

ST: The Bosnian sections are perhaps about the absence of love.

EE: Right, but it's the hunger for love, and the pain of someone who's suffered from hate.

ST: Do you see your work at all as similar at all to the work that Anna Deavere Smith is doing?

EE: We work very, very differently. I've seen two or three of her shows. She's in the first place an actress, which I'm not.

ST: You don't consider yourself an actress?

EE: No. I'm performing *The Vagina Monologues*. I go in, I interview people, I hear their stories and then I let them go through me and it becomes something else. I've worked this way for the last 20 years. Anna Deavere Smith takes people's stories and says them just the way she hears them. She doesn't turn it into quote unquote art. Her process with it may be artistic, but it's documentation: here's this, here's this, here's this. That's not what I do. I go in and I hear the stories and then they become mine.

ST: Do you consider yourself a documentarian at all?

EE: No.

ST: No?

EE: No. Because what I tell people when I interview them is "I'm going to listen to your story, then I'm going to take it, then I'm going to turn it into something else. And that's what I need your permission for. I'm not going to just say your story the way you told it to me." It's interviewing people to get the gist and get a kind of general truth about something. But then I take the liberties to change language, to invent, to embellish, to make it theater.

ST: To make it art.

EE: Yeah. Documenting doesn't necessarily make it art. There's a raised level of consciousness or awareness to art that's different than documentation. And that interests me a lot.

ST: Right. Well, what's the relationship between humor and the deep human truths that you're trying to get at in your work?

EE: Look, everything is so painful. Let's face it. Everything is so painful. The human condition is so painful. Is there anything about it that's not painful?

ST: No!

EE: We are born, which is painful. We get sick, which is painful. We get old, which is painful. And then we die. Those are the four sufferings. It's a lot of pain. In between that, we have enormous loss, we suffer incredible heartbreak, we are betrayed constantly. I'm not a negative person. I mean, this is life. There are also incredibly wonderful things that occur. I know that what saved me was being able to laugh at it, being able to go, "Yep. It's awful and it's the most absurd." Like being in refugee camps, or being in homeless shelters, or being in prisons, the one unvarying thing you see is humor. The places of the worst atrocity are always the places of the greatest humor, because it's how people survive. And without that, I don't know how you keep going on. Humor is a lifeboat. It's an absurd gift in the face of incredible horrors that we're facing all the time. And if we could somehow learn to keep laughing, it also joins us. There's a way in which humor builds community. Where anger, it seems to me, is very separating, unless people are angry together, but even then I'm not sure it's a bonding emotion. It can be, but often it isolates you. If people can laugh together, they can do anything together. So, um, I think everything that is revolutionary is funny. You know? Humor is revolutionary.

ST: What are the kinds of things that you find funny?

EE: I have a very dark sense of humor, as you may have noted in the work. I find things funny where everything is utterly hopeless and then there's this great absurd thing that occurs in the middle of it.

ST: *Waiting for Godot* comes to mind.

EE: Exactly. Beckett is hysterically funny. What I find funny is when—I'll tell you a great story, a crazy story. I went to Tibet. The altitude there is scary, as you know. People can get really sick. They tell you when you get there, "Don't exert yourself because if you exert yourself, something terrible can happen to you." So, we went to this amazing, amazing place. We had to take this ancient wooden boat across this mud river; really, it was like the river of the unconscious. There were these men with long beards steering the boat. When we got to the other side, there was this truck, and it was a truck for migrant workers, and you have to stand and hold on in the back of it. Our guide said, "Why don't you sit up front?" and I said, "No, I can do this." A true macho woman. So, I had to hold on with all my might for an hour over bumpy, bumpy roads, and when we got to the monastery, I felt like I was going to die. I was spinning, I had altitude sickness, I was vomiting. I've never been so sick in my life. I was bending over this ancient stone, where the first monastery had been established. All these Tibetan boys were watching me. And all these dogs, who are seen as reincarnated monks, around them. And I'm dying. My partner was there, and I was like, "Uhhhh." I am dying and vomiting, and out of nowhere, I farted. I don't know why. I just farted. But I have to tell you, those little boys went insane with laughter, to the point where they were crying, holding themselves. My partner was on the ground. It was so absurd that something changed in my whole system. I started to laugh. And through laughing, I stopped throwing up. I got okay. To me that is a perfect role for humor. Where everything is utterly awful, you're at the end of the world, you've traveled to Tibet, your life is destroyed, you're about to vomit and die, everyone is staring at you as you're vomiting and dying, there's no place to go, there's no way out, and then you fart. When I can create a moment like that, there's nothing better.

ST: Even unintentionally.

EE: But you have to be careful not to get cheap with humor because you can start to use it as a way of avoiding stuff. The truth is to find ways to deepen with humor as opposed to escape with it. There are a lot of writers who escape with humor, which I don't have much interest in. Whenever I feel like I'm being taken away from the pain, taken away from the subject, taken away from the corpse, humor doesn't interest me. But I feel like humor, with Beckett or Pinter, is bringing it closer to the subject. Then, it's like, "Yes!"

ST: Humor can also be used as a way of controlling, which is related to what you're saying. It can be a way of not going where it's too scary to go.

EE: I love dark humor, where you're constantly tumbling deeper into the abyss. But there's a lot of humor that I don't like, that I find cute or precious.

ST: Whose work do you read? Are there other writers and playwrights whose work you seek out?

EE: The greatest inspirations for me, in terms of writers, have been Tennessee Williams, Beckett, Pinter, and Brecht. Those are the people who have influenced my work the most. As novelists go, that's a whole different world with writers like Toni Morrison and Virginia Woolf. In terms of playwrights, I also love Caryl Churchill. But Beckett is my favorite playwright, without a doubt. There's a way in which he's able to be absurd and funny and philosophical, all at the same time.

ST: And to bring us in.

EE: Absolutely. And stripped raw communicating, in the flesh of it.

ST: In *The Vagina Monologues* you're forging new territory with your work. Do you see it fitting into a particular tradition?

EE: Not really. Women playwrights write differently. Our concerns are different. Our voices are different. Our structure is different. Our styles are different. And we're very new, in playwriting. And, not like women haven't been writing for centuries, but because we have been given so little space and so little recognition and so little opportunity that we're just beginning to break into this forum in our way. The Greeks have also had an incredible affect on me. Aristophanes, and *Electra*, and— That's why I started writing plays because there's a kind of pure emotional world that women know that is very theatrical. And it interests me a lot. *The Vagina Monologues* definitely explores that. *Necessary Targets*, the Bosnia play, does, too. It looks at emotion in a very naked, concentrated way.

ST: I'm sure you've noticed this, but so many people apologize when they say the word "vagina." I became conscious of this when I knew that I was going to be talking to you. I thought, "Let's drop it. Let's drop the apology and start saying the word. Vagina, vagina, vagina." I've been having great conversations with people about this.

EE: When you apologize for having a vagina, what are you apologizing for? Being alive, essentially. It's like apologizing for crying. Why do people say that they're sorry when they're crying? What is that? It's like saying you're sorry that you're coming. I'm happy that I can cry. I feel good that I've worked on my system enough that I can cry, that I'm not all blocked up and stuffed up.

ST: You don't want the standard to be no emotion, no sexuality, no anything.

EE: Neuter, dead, dumb. No!

ST: Is there anything that you would like to add? Anything that we haven't covered about humor or about your work?

EE: Mainly the whole idea is that humor is another way in. It's another path. An essential path. And you have to trust your politics, and trust your voice, which will communicate through humor, as opposed to you putting your voice on top of things.

ST: What about your timing? Is that innate?

EE: Who knows!

ST: Part of humor is knowing when to be silent, too.

EE: There's a moment in the Bob piece [see accompanying *Vagina Monologue*], which goes, "I imagined things between my legs. I imagined furniture." I can feel the beat of it. Now if you say, "I imagined furniture," it's not funny. If you say, "I imagined [*beat*] furniture," you get the laugh.

ST: That's true.

EE: Now, why that is? Every night I experiment and I can say the same line and I can get a huge laugh one way and no laugh the other. It's the way you put things together—and the nuance, the accent, or where you emphasize something. It's so much fun discovering what that is. What is it that makes people laugh?

ST: It's a little mysterious.

EE: I'll give you an example from *The Vagina Monologues*, where the six-year-old girl says, in answer to "If your vagina could talk, what would it say?" She says, "It would say words that begin with 'V' and 'T.' Turtle and violin are examples." Now, in the original thing, she did not say, "are examples." She said, "Like turtle and violin." That's not funny. But when you say, "Turtle and violin are examples," that's really funny.

ST: It is really funny.

EE: Now why?

ST: I don't know. It must have something to do with the specificity of the language.

EE: Absolutely. It's very exact. Discovering what is funny is so much fun. There's a great book by Henri Bergson called *Laughter*. It's a wonderful, wonderful book on philosophy and laughter. I did this project in college on that book. It influenced me deeply. Our exercise for the class was to come in and make someone laugh and then we would analyze why we laughed. I remember I came into class with a brown paper bag over my head and sat through the whole class. And people were hysterical. And then we had a whole discussion about "Why is that funny? What about that moment is funny?" It's so interesting to break apart the moment and see what that is.

Senso's Diary

by Megan Ratner

By dint of sheer good luck (and two dinners at the always-booked Kundalini Grill), Director's Chair *secured the following blow-by-blow chronicle from indie sensation Senso Unico on the making of his "Pater Patter," the no-holds-barred diary of the first year of his daughter Kurosawa's life. Excerpts are from* Siring Pater Patter, *forthcoming from Im Press.*

—THE EDITORS

June 5/March 30

Two dates: the first when we became pregnant (in Albania!—lots of shooting but got good deal on hotel), the second when Kurosawa appeared (in TriBeCa). June 5 her conception and, although I didn't realize it at the time, the conception of the film: two very important moments in great scheme.

Am filled with love for courageous Ursula, with lust for life, with sense of importance in universe.

Why want to screw every woman in sight?

March 31

Kurosawa's first day. She has eyes of old soul, ancient and knowing. Already feel guilty around her. Enormous shopping for all baby equipment—like financing entire film. Suppose this normal.

Bad sign that Ursula pushed her away after feeding? Wish she would get excited about film.

April 6

K. one week old, I'm one week older. This must be how snake feels shedding skin: K. born, I reborn.

Found Lars filming during off-hours, extra footage of U. sleeping. Big argument. Can't afford to use film that way, he should know after being with me on "Hostile Hostels." Ego very difficult. People mostly impossible. Have to make sure K. not so.

undated

Found U. nibbling at K.'s fingernails. Said she was afraid to cut, thought chewing off better, more control. Lars filmed whole episode, fight also. Good for project, bad for real life—felt terrible for afternoon. Cut in final?

May 1

Am really a daddy now—even go to park. People want to know why K.'s name Japanese. One mother insulted because her daughter is adopted Chinese—maybe she'd be happier if K. named Gong Li. Mothers not willing to be filmed for PP. Very competitive, worried their children won't come off as well as K. Fatherhood dangerous as any other 'hood.

May 13

Terrific meeting with Bernie Lipetsk, ready to bankroll entire project. Complained of predictability of lawyering. Holding glass of beaujolais nouveau, he said, "Like this wine, you *est arrivée*." U. unimpressed and still a little cool towards K.

May 30

Mem. Day fest here, lots of old buddies, grilling on rooftop, general mayhem. K. a big hit, only U. not interested. Bernie a little smashed, kept telling people, "I love this guy."

Carried K. in snuggly all day, U. gone for long period. Lars also.

New perspective on mortality with K. around: Methuselah now role model.

June 10

Found out mothers changed play group date without telling me. Am only stay-at-home dad in area and feel betrayed. Even when mothers, women deceptive.

K. great, as always. Pretty sure began to say da-da.

July 3

U. heading Upstate without K. Feel it's too soon. U. told me to put it in film, didn't care. Obviously motherhood not as meaningful to her as f-hood to me. Lars gone, unreachable. Had to get dreaded cameraman Tod, annoying, but film must go on. K. adorable.

July 27

Call from Mom—in hospital and wants visit. Worst timing. Once parents start aging, no stopping them. Sent Marika. Mom likes, though Marika annoyed—says not part of assistant job.

August 6

Hiroshima destroyed today in 1945. My life ruined right now. U. incommunicado, Lars definitely with her. K. lovely but being single parent TOO MUCH.

Mom better, out of intensive care. Finally. Filmed sequence on her thoughts on being grandmother. Not as positive as I'd like—Mom still mad that I want Marika back. Even thinks K. looks more like U. than me.

August 29

U. back, lukewarm with K., even though not seen for more than month. U.'s only answer to questions about future/relationship is "I don't know." Bernie wants to make preemptive strike, ensure custody for me. No baby, no movie. K. very cute but lots of work. Marika not happy at new nanny duties. Mom calling all the time.

Why all women unhappy?

September 16

Great day! Bernie hooked up with Gareth Spindle who wants to distribute PP! I'm staying at Maison de la Casa in L.A., in same bungalow they gave Ingmar. Can feel moody vibe.

U. dim memory, apparently back Upstate, alone this time.

September 22

Came back to disaster. Phone not working even after changed all fuses in apartment. Found unpaid bill. U. determined to wreck me, wreck project.

October 3

Wow, what a break! Lars back on team. Got amazing footage of U. unaware of camera, positioned just to side of full-length mirror as she assesses post-pregnancy body, discusses me and K.

Am so insightful—knew she didn't like motherdom.

Risky to put in final. Love it.

October 25

Invitation to Berlin if film done. Wish I could make K. grow a little faster—seems to have plateaued. Also listless.

November 27

Thanksgiving. Grateful for K., Mom, Marika. Lars, too, though demanding co-creator credit for U. footage. Very low, really.

Mom feeble, had to rest after meal—hope doesn't die before film done. Can't possibly work deathbed visits in with post-production.

10 December

Why holidays? Big pain to have to stop and party when I'm so deep into film. K. really natural, more energized again.

Took to see psychic who said ancient eyes part of whole ancient personality—K. actually old soul. Psychic unsure as to who or what but sure this is not K.'s first time around.

December 31

K. best of last year. U. leaving worst.

January 3

Lars and I agree on U.—self-centered and pitiless. Hope K. has more of my DNA.

Mom weak and sickly. Back in hospital indefinitely. Marika coming through, big help. She and Lars very good with K.

February 14

Close to wrapping up shooting. Feeling nostalgic for infant days. K. walking, almost talking. Much more own person. Sad. Would like K. to remain infant; finally understand foot binding—too bad only works on foot.

February 20

Worried. Find K. pretty dull. Not learning shapes and colors very fast. Learning problems to come? U. wants money to enroll in massage course. Mom complaining again re: old age. She's 75. Why not used to it by now?

March 1

Film going very well. Newest development: Marika and Lars. Seem very happy. Lars filmed me discussing my jealousy of their love. K. being cute but same old, same old with her. Am experiencing f-hood fatigue.

March 2–3

Sneaked away for ashram weekend. Just what needed. Took C., a new friend met at Sundance last year. She now divorced also. Exciting.

Didn't miss K.

March 5

A full year, Kurosawa walking. Feel time right for change. Marika and Lars moving in together, want to take K. Bernie drew up agreement—can see K. whenever I have time.

Beginning of life passé. Death real cutting edge.

Mom looks promising—am working on video-monitored coffin...

Coitus Hysterium

by Rebecca McClanahan

If some statistician were looking
on, charting the number of times
we up or down the national average,
this coupling might confuse him.

We are not the Joneses
or the Johnsons, simply masters
in the art of married laughter,
and another position we sometimes take

in love is flat on our backs,
spending ourselves in knee slaps
and shrieks to the bedroom wall.
We never intend to go this far,

but things get quickly out of hand,
out of even your brilliant hands
which after twenty-plus years never
fail to answer my body's question.

You are a puppeteer skilled
in sleight, your slightest tug
can make me dance and throw
my voice so far it may still

be singing somewhere.
This is not counting, certainly
not discounting the seamier joys
of married trysts, those numberless

permutations of pleasure
one man and one woman take
and give. Nor the times when loss
or circumstance has lashed us

together and we've wept
at the lastness of things, washing
ashore on broken bodies. Yes,
any shadow hovering recasts

the scene below. But tonight let's not
praise the buzz-saw of passion,
the thin edge that could razor
one couple into separate strands.

There's something to be said
for the thrust and rhythm
of a joke well told, the orgasmic
wave of a belly laugh solving

the body's other riddle. *Knock, knock,*
I whisper, breathless in the silence
I count on you to break in two,
your hands in the dark moving

beyond lust to cup
the answer, the quilled titillation
of your mustache against
my ear: *Who's there?*

The Hand

by Rebecca McClanahan

Pointer

Nose-picker, harvester of navel lint
and what the scrawny boy prays for at recess,
standing by the bleachers. *You* and *you* and *you,*
God dividing the goats from the lambs.
And *you*—the terrorist's finger singles you out.
It's come with me, the woman in the red dress,
death angel, invitation, the finger crooked and calling,
and what the blind witch asked to touch before Gretel's
chicken bone trick. It's the finger an angry mother raises,
louder than her voice. The one the nurse pricks
to smear on the slide. The finger you lick before you flip
through a phone book, the one that knows the way. Magical
dactyl,
(a curse on you, a pox!) And on your lips, shh—
the mystery, secret kept, the finger in the dike.

Middle

Digitus obscenus. Longest, biggest
papa of them all. Jupiter, Saturn,
and what the Roman temple whores
wrote with in midair: Pen, penis, peak,
pinnacle of the mountain my hands make

in prayer. And behind my back, the protector
that mates with Pointer when I lie.

Ring Finger

Wrapped in a bloody kerchief, it's the one kidnappers
mail home. Slender and limp, a willing victim, the prettiest
finger of all. A love-vein flows directly from this finger
to the heart, making it the Venus trap, bonbon wife.
Husbands often leave it bare, claiming fear
of dismemberment, but in truth it's the one
we'd miss least of all, weak-kneed pupil the piano teacher
coaxes with a ruler when it swoons upon the keys.

Little Finger

Pinky O Pinky, how we love you, little lambkins.
Cute as a button. Would you curtsy for us again?

Thumb

There's one in every family: dumb
mutant missing a link. Biologists say
it makes us who we are—graspers, users,
a weapon in each hand. You or the lion?
Thumbs down, you lose. Thumbs up, the hammer
will find you. All thumbs? It's a stumpy job,
but someone's got to do it. Swollen tumor
the size of the soul, and its dance is the heart beating.
Maybe that's the charm of this lumpy child—
Hop-O-My-Thumb, Thumbelina—who,

joined with Pointer, forms the Yogi's circle,
the universal okay. Don't worry.
If all else fails, you can always hitch a ride
back to Mama, or suck it till it's dry.

Teaching My Computer Dirty Words

by Rebecca McClanahan

Learn, I command, and tap the key
that will commit to its digital memory
the necessary *shits* and *goddamns*
(now the terrified man
in my story can finally *piss* blood)

and this from a woman
whose childhood lips tightened
on *Jeepers Creepers* and *Jiminy Cricket,*
certain they were the vain
takings of Someone's name,

a child who pronounced helicopter
with a long *e* for fear of bringing *hell*
down upon her ears, which she covered
like the third no-evil monkey,
and still shields against rappers

and pubescents for whom *fuck*
is a punctuation mark, rendering
the once potent single engine pump
useless in emergencies. Like a child,
should a computer be taught

when and where to spew with impunity?
Once the words enter, a machine
will never question.
I imagine it tasting
each new obscenity, rolling it around
on its silicon tongue, weighing the heft,

the consonantal snap and click,
the way my young nephews,
having recently discovered *fart,*
chant it like a mantra, some holy
abracadabra that will open

the jewel box of Anglo Saxon
satisfactions. My word was *damn.*
For years I carried it inside my mouth
while it hummed like a bee
demanding out. Aside from the Bible

I'd heard it only twice—my father
slamming the hood on the stalled Chevy,
my aunt in stubbed toe misery.
A word so rare must be hoarded, I decided,
for a special occasion of pain or anger,

and when both presented themselves
simultaneously, some blond boy
doing me public wrong, I let fly
a mouthful that stung the air
yellow, oh the power of venom

released. Thus I explain to the computer
how sometimes only profanity
will suffice. Horror and ugliness
demand their own yard, as does each
deadly sin. "The captives were forced..."

the story begins, "to eat their own..."
what? *Excrement* cannot begin
to feed their world, nor should *love*
be confused with the hardwood
headboard one-syllable rams

that, yes, we all at one time
or another require. Go ahead,
I tell the keyboard, bang the words
in and out of your system until they explode
into compound constellations—unspeakable

things to do to mothers and roosters,
twofold mythological constructions
(Dickhead, Shitface) for renaming
friends and family. Like Eve go ahead
and name the animal inside us,

without which our history
could not be written, our palates
cleansed to receive the sacrament
(how excellent is Thy name in all the earth)
of bread or pleasure, so when we type

penis, we are singing the sacred
tail of delight, and with it the vulval
flower, its clefts and folds,
the perfect inclination of clitoral
hill, the fraternal Labial twins

someone named Majora and Minora
like the bivalved world
that encloses us, a world that takes us
whole, or not at all, into its mouth,
the spoiled and unspoiled garden.

Apprenticeship

by Bob Slaymaker

Before running for office,
to perfect the art of lying,
so crucial to a career in government,
you must first work many years
in a small Manhattan store—
a pizzeria, donut shop or deli—
where every ten minutes you are asked
by a tight-lipped customer,
"Do you have a bathroom?"
To which you must reply,
with sincerity and a straight face,
"No."
Only after years of this kind of deceit
are you equal to the task of politics.

Sapience

by Stan Friedman

Beneath a tyrannosaurus, two boys
Go at it. Neither of them
Half the size of the mastodon's drumstick,
They kick, pull hair and scream,
Their nostrils flaring. Only the living
Are unsettled, there is such little power
In their chubby frames, not even the bones
Of the creature's smallest toe vibrate.
"Don't ever touch me again!" the blond one
With a bloody nose shouts. He is too
Primitive to see the luxury of his words.
He says "ever" like he never heard
Of extinction, as though this room of skeletons
Is just for show.

Strolling past a glass-encased rhino,
A man tugs at his wife's hair and whispers,
"look Hon, it's your sister."
She doesn't laugh. The baby is kicking
And her new hugeness breeds
Only pity for the obese girl
Who once taught her to walk
On her hands. She pretends
To observe the animal but her glassy eyes

Make it obvious she is scanning
Her own reflection. And when she finally
Does crack a smile, it is because
She knows that he is the rhino,
A phallus growing out his forehead,
Where it belongs.

A whale is suspended from the ceiling. I stand
Under the massive arc of its blue gut,
Uneaten. Luckier than Jonah, I am
Relatively ignorant of how it feels
To be swallowed into darkness, and yes,
I am better off than this whale.
Still, like any mammal, I can sense fear
And now I smell it in my own musk,
The paranoia, peculiar to my species,
That the beast will come crashing down,
And worse, in the second before I vanish,
I might understand how my history ends.

A Brush With Desire

by Stan Friedman

She's biting down and
licking his nose she's tied
his feet with her bra his hands
with her hose he's bouncing
into her laughing uncontrollably
fragrant lust-rotten guffaws,
her whispers hot cuss words
their steam rising to his nostrils
like coke then a scissor
of light, a cloak, strikes from under
her mane from beneath
the pillow itself reveals
a pair of wings gossamer
as the bubble of spit inflating
on his lips and Shit! it's
the Tooth Fairy risen
from his childhood bed (now
of all times) to redeem
the cuspid he would not surrender
that he tried to glue back
but ended up swallowing and
the woman is blaring clawing
his back the imp not even
embarrassed as it frees itself

waving a wand and she yells
there's no such thing
it was your mom
late at night he is having
an orgasm and a halo
of stars spins around the wand
he feels the hollow in his gut
conks out till daybreak
when she and it and it
are gone his limbs still bound
a silver dollar wedged
between his knees.

THOUSANDS OF YOU HAVE ALREADY BENEFITED FROM our fast selling book, *The Rules,* and are well on your way to the altar. But for those who are still searching for Mr. Right, we've provided an addendum to Rule 31. Take note and take heart girls, your future husband could be sitting right across from you.

Addendum to Rule 31:

Don't Tell Your Therapist About *The Rules*, Do *The Rules* on Your Therapist!

by Meghan Daum

Your therapist must be viewed not as someone to whom you blab out every little thing but as another person who might want to marry you. This being the case, play hard to get, leave him wanting more, show up late to sessions or don't show up at all. Refuse to pay for these missed sessions (remember, *Rules* girls never pay.) Make sure he's dying to see you every week, dressing extra nice on your day, stalling at the end of the session so he can have more time with you. Don't say anything that will make you seem pathetic or desperate. Don't reveal too much personal information or whine about things that happened in your childhood. This will only make him think you are a negative person, which is the opposite of what *Rules* girls should be.

Always be happy and cheerful and make sure that you are dressed sexily without looking like a hooker. A particularly alluring look for therapy is a brightly colored, v-neck top and a miniskirt that you can hitch up as you lie on the couch. Make sure you wear sheer black stockings without any runs. Shoes are important, since you are lying down and he will be able to see them, so don't cut corners. Try not to wear the same outfit more than once every eight weeks if you go once a week or once every month if you go twice a week. Remember that the therapist, unlike other men you may have been interested in, has no way of seeing your apartment and therefore has no clues to your personal style other than your clothes and hair (which should be long). So dress with care! When you write checks to him, be sure that your handwriting is neat and feminine, not jagged and sloppy. If this means setting aside extra time to write checks calmly and with your best pen, give yourself that time. Remember that this is the penmanship that will be used to answer invitations to social engagements and write notes to your children's teachers when you are married, so it counts! No man wants a wife who scrawls like a doctor. Anyway, he's the doctor. You might also consider ordering special checks that have flowers or an attractive border, which will show that you have a certain flair.

If your therapist suggests that you start coming more often, give yourself a little pat on the back. *The Rules* are working! Still, you must play it cool. Tell him that you can't come more often because you've "got a million things to do." Make him woo you into coming more often. Only after he has begged and pleaded with you to come twice a week should you accept (remembering to be late as often as possible). If he ever tries to reschedule, make sure he gives you at least four days notice, otherwise you're certainly not available. You, however, should reschedule all the time. See how much he'll juggle his calendar to accommodate you. You have a life, make sure he knows it. You're busy going to the gym and to parties. When you have time on your hands you do not sit around thinking about your therapist. You do some sit-ups or read a magazine to brush up on the latest fashion tips. You get a manicure so your nails will be perfect the next time you go to therapy. Use your hands (in moderation) when you talk so he will notice your left ring finger and imagine what it would look like with a huge diamond on it.

Let your therapist do most of the talking, remembering to interject things like "that's so interesting" and "I'll bet you're wonderful at your job" at appropriate moments. Often therapists will pry and try to get you to reveal things about yourself that you would rather not go into until you've reached a serious commitment. Be strong and do not allow this. The idea is to be mysterious and unknowable. Never talk about previous relationships. If you once had a drinking problem, don't say anything about it. If your mother locked you in a closet when you were eight, keep it to yourself. In fact, don't say anything critical about your mother. You do, after all, want him to consider her an appealing candidate for a future mother-in-law. If he specifically asks you about her and you have nothing good to say, tell him that she has a lovely garden and keep it at that. In general, it's best to deflect the conversation away from yourself. Find out what his hobbies are and get him to talk about them (this may require some extra research on your part but don't let him know that). For example, if he was away for the month of August you can casually ask him what he was doing (and we mean casually, *Rules* girls are never too interested). If he says he was at a psychoanalytic conference in Denver, you can ask him how the weather was in Denver. Don't pretend to be an expert in his field.

Soon enough, your therapist will start calling you at home "just to talk." Only when he has called you five times should you call him back and talk for no longer than ten minutes. As always, you should be the one to end the call. A good line to use is "I'm afraid our time is up." Even if your therapist is the man of your dreams and you find it painful and difficult to do *The Rules* where he's concerned, you must keep doing *The Rules*. If the years go by and you feel you are getting nowhere, you might have to terminate therapy. Of course, you're not really leaving him. As a *Rules* girl, you know exactly what you're doing. He will be so devastated that he'll do anything to get you back, showering you with jewelry, even dropping his other patients if necessary. At that point, you can resume your treatment with the understanding that you now have a serious commitment. You will no doubt find that in time, usually within two to ten years, your therapist will fall madly in love with you and propose.

Castro Convertible Girl

by Kate Moira Ryan

SCENE I

(*T.V. music. A twelve-year-old girl named Chi Chi Castro in a long flowing dress skips on stage. She opens a sofa bed, gets into the bed, snuggles down sleepily and then the bed begins to close and the girl screams as she is crushed to death.*)

SCENE II

(*Early the next morning. Same girl bolts up in her Castro Convertible bed. She looks around, takes her pillow and blanket and sleeps on the floor.*)

SCENE III

(*Chi Chi having her makeup done by her mother Big Chi Chi. Little Chi Chi is holding a cigarette and chewing gum.*)

CHI CHI: Mah, I don't want to do this no more.

B.C.C.: (*Slaps her.*) Stop moving, Chi Chi. How am I supposed to put on your makeup while you're twitching your facial cartilage, huh? Give me Oo! Oo! surprise eyebrows. (*Chi Chi raises her eyebrows.*) Good baby, now give me Shirley Temple apple cheeks. (*Chi Chi smiles maniacally.*)

CHI CHI: Mah, you're not listening. I don't want to be on T.V. no more.

B.C.C.: (*Takes the cigarette from little Chi Chi's hand and takes a drag and then hands it back.*) Look, I was a Castro convertible girl, Ula was a Castro convertible girl. It's tradition. It's a honor. You rather your fat cousin Rosalita should have the national instead of you? You want to kill your grandfather, huh?

CHI CHI: I've been having the dreams again.

B.C.C.: Your sister, may God be giving her kisses, lollipops, and all the Barbies that she wants, was an unfortunate accident.

CHI CHI: I know, but...

B.C.C.: Didn't your grandfather pull the Castro automatic off the market after that?

CHI CHI: I know, but what about what happened to your leg?

B.C.C.: I didn't have the eye hand coordination needed for the job.

CHI CHI: What about Ula?

B.C.C.: It says right on the mattress tag, "Do not operate while under the influence of alcohol or decongestants." I should have read the back of that Sudafed package.

CHI CHI: But...

B.C.C.: No more and, if's or but's. You'll do as your grandmother, mother and late sister did. You're a Castro Convertible girl. It's your fate. Now let's see your skip. C'mon! (*She slaps her hands together. Chi Chi skips across the floor.*) Again, put your hips into it. We're not selling children's Tylenol here.

SCENE IV

(*Night. Chi Chi is skipping around the sofa. She turns the skip into a run. The sofa catches her by the edge of her night dress and begins to chew her slowly until her night gown is ripped off. One of the arms of the sofa begins fondling her. Chi Chi tries to resist. She is thrown on the sofa, pinned down, and the cushions molest her. She screams. Blackout.*)

SCENE V

(*Day. Big Chi Chi is working with a script with Little Chi Chi. Little Chi Chi is dazed. She holds her mother's cigarette and occasionally takes a drag herself.*)

B.C.C.: Now Abuelo Castro called me last night. He has a designed a new model that he wants you to demonstrate. Okay? Hey, Chi Chi (*slaps her on the head*). You been eating paint chips again?

CHI CHI: The sofa's been messing with me.

B.C.C.: What do you mean messing with you?

CHI CHI: It's been touching me in my private parts like Uncle Carlo…

B.C.C.: You been eating paint chips again. You're hallucinating.

CHI CHI: I haven't eaten paint chips since I was three. I'm twelve now and the Castro convertible was messing with me last night. Messing with me so that I'm sore inside. Sore.

B.C.C.: You don't like the product fine. Fine, but don't make up lies about the product. Don't.

CHI CHI: I'm not making up lies.

B.C.C.: You resemble the cousin we don't talk about.

CHI CHI: That's not true!

B.C.C.: I should put you on a boat and send you there.

CHI CHI: NO!

B.C.C.: One more thing, Chi Chi, and I'm sending yah to Fidel in an inner tube. Understand? I said, do you understand yah commie pink brat?

CHI CHI: Yeah.

B.C.C.: Alright, grandpa wants you do a skip and dip around the sofa before opening it. Watch me. (*She noticeably limps while she does an ornate skip and dip with lots of sexual innuendos around the sofa. Chi Chi miserably follows her.*)

SCENE VI

(*Night. Little Chi Chi is pregnant and skipping around the sofa with hysterical and frantic motion. Suddenly, she clutches her stomach, drops onto the sofa and goes into labor. She gives birth to a tiny Castro convertible. She begins to scream.*)

SCENE VII

(*Little Chi Chi is lying on the floor in a fetal position. She sucks her thumb. Offstage Big Chi Chi is talking to Ula.*)

B.C.C.: I can't do nothing with her. She don't want to skip no more. She won't sleep on her sofa bed. And the lies she tells about the product, ay bendito! (*Pause and then whispers.*) She says that the sofa has been messing with her. (*Pause.*) Violating her. (*Pause.*) Like been touching her privates. (*Pause.*) Doing SEXUAL THINGS! SHE'S BEEN SAYING THE SOFA'S BEEN RAPING HER, like Carlo used to when she was a kid. (*Pause.*) I always knew Carlo was a sick fuck, but family's family. I'd rather have her perverted Uncle playing doctor with the kid than some stranger off the street. Anyways, I can't do nothing with little Chi Chi. She don't want to do the commercials no more. All she wants to do lay there like a soggy taco. I was hoping Papa that you could do something with her. You how she fears you...Nough said.

(Offstage. A Tootsie Roll is pelted at Little Chi Chi. Then another and another.)

CHI CHI: Ow! Abuelo?

(A very old man who keeps on aiming Tootsie Rolls at Chi Chi walks in. He is wearing a big fedora hat and smoking a cigar.)

ABUELO: Where is my little Chi Chi? *(He throws another and hits Chi Chi.)*

CHI CHI: OUCH!

(He walks in her direction and then trips over her. Chi Chi helps him up and leads him over to the sofa bed. They sit down.)

Abuelo, sit here.

ABUELO: I hit you with your favorite, Tootsie Rolls.

CHI CHI: That was my dead sister's favorite. I like to be hit with Jolly Ranchers.

ABUELO: Now what's this, little Chi Chi? What's this about you not wanting to be the Castro Convertible girl anymore?

CHI CHI: I have these dreams. I have these nightmares about the Castro Convertible sofa bed. They seem so real.

ABUELO: Your mother says that you've been saying that the sofa's been for want of a better word penetrating you. That what you dream about?

CHI CHI: Yes, Abuelo and I feel so, so unclean.

ABUELO: Ci, Ci, Ci. Little Chi Chi, I understand.

CHI CHI: You do?

ABUELO: When I was a little boy in Cuba, we didn't make sofa beds, we made hammocks. Each night, I would go to sleep in the hammock and I would dream that the hammock was strangling me. I would wake up and the hammock would be all twisted around me. I would tell my mama and pappy that the hammock was messing with me. They beat me and they beat me. They thought that I was lying. The nightmares got worse until I could only sleep on the ground.

CHI CHI: What did you do?

ABUELO: Well, I got me a pair of scissors and one night, I laid in the hammock and waited for the dream to come.

CHI CHI: And?

ABUELO: And when the dream came, I slashed that goddamn hammock to shreds.(*He pulls out a pair of very old scissors and hands them to Little Chi Chi.*) It made me a man. It will make you a woman. Go slay the sofa, Chi Chi, and get a good night's sleep. (*He walks away.*)

SCENE VIII

(*That night. Chi Chi lies in the sofa bed asleep. The sofa slowly begins to attack her again. Chi Chi wakes up within her dream and begins to tentatively fight back with the scissors. The sofa fights back. Chi Chi goes berserk and slaughters the sofa until it no longer moves.*)

SCENE IX

(*Next morning. Chi Chi wakes up from a good night's sleep. She jumps up and skips around the sofa. She trips. And looks at the sofa with some measure of trepidation. Then she gets up with great resolve, hits the sofa on the arm and skips along merrily.*)

The Fat Boy

by Scott Ferguson

Right, but you can't care about it. Shut up, that word's not in my lexicon, nor in my sexy condo. Yes but the police said you're not allowed to mean it. Yes but I say in France a spooky French girl naps. Oh yes I think I see where you mean now the how you say red light area. It's there my soul, long-discredited, was discarded. Suddenly there was scrollwork and fancy, partial facades.

The rebel pose partly fades or is adumbrated. Take up your hockey skates, quell the radioplaying in widows' houses. I might have known him in a way or in rain. Refer to page 337, negated, erased, wind's plaything. Mother-love keeps sustaining ships and bison in dioramas.

He Looked at Me Funny

by Johnnie Morello

IN THE LAST FIVE YEARS A FRIEND OF MINE HAS MOVED from New York to LA to San Francisco to Phoenix to Sante Fe to West Palm Beach. He called recently. I asked how he was.

"Right now I'm juggling a lot of balls in the air," he said, "and two of them are *mine.* I'll let you know when they come down."

And I thought, "Hmmm. Another guy with only two balls." Unless he's got others he's not juggling. But I didn't think that was the case.

I'd been thinking about my own balls lately. They were on my mind. They felt as if I'd been juggling *them,* and not too well at that. One of them hurt and I was considering going to the doctor. I'd never put much faith in the medical profession unless they were telling me that I didn't have cancer. The last time I'd gone to a doctor was for heart pains and I was very nervous. The guy looked at me.

"You don't have heart trouble," he said.

"Could you run some tests?"

"Sure," he said. "We can run some tests. We can run as many tests as you want. How much do you wanna spend?"

Naturally, I didn't want to spend anything and told him as much. He charged me forty dollars, but the pains went away. Cured. That was two years ago.

So I made an appointment. It was at a hospital clinic upstate. Actually, it was upstate and over to the left, which made it out of state. I thought it would be easier there. I guess I didn't trust anybody in New York City with my balls.

I drove the long drive to the hospital. A nurse ushered me into the examination room where I sat for a long time, waiting for the doctor. I looked around closely but could find nothing worth stealing. I guess they were hip to that. The doctor finally burst in. I was wondering where he'd been but I didn't ask. He was a young guy, my age. I was hoping he'd know a lot about balls. Although we were up and out of state, I was still paying good money. As usual, he checked my ears first. I don't know why. Someday I'm gonna ask that.

"What seems to be the problem?" he said. I was hoping he'd be more creative, but now, at least I knew he was a real doctor.

"One of my balls hurts." I figured let's cut right to the chase.

"Hm," he said. "You want to take your pants down please? And get up on the table."

"Whatever happened to romance?" I thought of saying, but I held it in. Then, anxious to help, I sacked the Doc's chance to experience the joy of true medical discovery.

"I have three balls," I said.

"Hmm," he said.

He acted as if his last patient had told him the same thing. His face didn't change. Much. But I could see that he was interested.

"That's one more than most people, isn't it?" I asked. Not that I couldn't remember but I was never really sure.

"Well, that's one more than most *men*, anyway," he said.

"Not bad," I thought, "but I'll get the laughs around here, Doc."

I knew he was cynical as he began groping.

"You can be as cynical as you want, Doc," I thought, "but you can count those suckers you can." I didn't say that either. I thought it. Figured I shouldn't wise off. After all, my balls were in his hands.

It had been on my mind a long time, this question of balls. And just how many should I have? I'd felt slighted by the medical profession. Dozens of physical examinations throughout my life. Each year a school physical. Family doctors. Army doctors. And no one had ever noticed. What were they doing when they grabbed me down there if not counting? Maybe they didn't care. Maybe they couldn't count! Perhaps I was a little shy. After all, I never said to any of these geniuses, "Did you notice I have three balls?" But why bother? They weren't hurting anyone. 'Til now. And it wasn't like me to ask another boy how many balls he had. That kind of thing might bring one's own balls under suspicion. And you know how kids can be.

Thinking back, I suppose I could have asked my health teacher how many balls do I have? But I don't think I had a health teacher. Once, some brave but unwitting kid said to me, "Y'know, between us we only have three balls?"

"Then I guess you don't have any," I said.

"No. I only have one nut," he said.

"Well I have three," I said to this barely nutted, nearly neutered fellow. "So between us we average two. The common denominator. Anybody questions you, stand next to me in the shower."

"Were you injured as a child?" Doc asks.

"Yes, I hurt my knee."

"In this area," he says, bringing me back to my balls.

"I was never hit hard enough to split my nuts in two," I tell him. I think of the atom. I remember a film strip I watched in the sixth grade.

Suddenly I recall or imagine that I once consulted a doctor about my condition and I tell the Doc about it.

"What did he say?" he asks, only half interested.

"He told me that one of them wasn't actually a testicle."

"This may hurt," the Doc says, further assuring me of his AMA credentials. And he's right. It does.

"I'm checking to see...," he says, too engrossed to finish his explanation. "I'm trying to find...," his words wander and he trails off again. "I want to see if they....all....funnel..."

"What?" I ask anxiously. My jewels are in his hands and I'm getting nervous.

"I want to see if they all have a Vas Deferens."

"Which is what?" I ask him.

He explains that it's a tube that leads up into whatever he says it leads up into.

"Do they?" I ask. "Do they all have one?"

"Um hm."

"So they're all..." I hope to prompt him. "...balls? They're all balls?"

"Yes," he announces. "They're all functioning testicles."

"Is this common?" I ask.

"No," he says, but he lacks the enthusiasm I'd hoped he'd have.

We pause. Two great minds are on my balls. Well, mine is anyway.

"Have you ever see it before?" I'm hoping he'll say no. This could be a real coup.

"No, I never have," he says.

"Hooray!" I say. "Should I pull my pants up?"

"Not yet," he says. "I want to talk to the endocrinologist and see what she thinks. Perhaps she'll have a look."

Oh boy! Another opinion! She? My lucky day. Some gorgeous endocrinologist is gonna come in and play with my balls. I look to see if there's a rheostat. The Doc is gone quite a while and I lay there on the table, propped up on one elbow, thinking about my balls.

When he finally returns, he is alone. I'm disappointed. I wanted to show my balls to someone else. I wanted to tell the world. I wanted to shout it from the rooftops; "I HAVE THREE FUNCTIONING TESTICLES!" But it wouldn't be the same without her. He said the endocrinologist had never heard of such a thing. Where is she then? World famous horny endocrinologist is too busy to check out a guy with three balls? Going once. Going twice. Forget it. I'm crestfallen. I picture her reading a book, just sitting there, under the weird pale light used to read x-rays. A *guy* would have come over. A guy *definitely* would have come over. To see this. They could talk about it at lunch tomorrow. They could make some funny remarks but then they would talk seriously about it. They might even put a photo of my balls in a medical journal, though I don't really have time for that sort of thing.

Maybe I shouldn't have gone out of state. This could have drawn a good crowd in New York. Anyway. The doctor tells me I have an infection. But, it's not life threatening. He actually says that. Not life threatening. He writes a prescription for an antibiotic that should fix me up. I feel some real satisfaction that it has been confirmed. I have three balls. I'm in the record book.

I shook hands with the doctor. I said, "You know, between us, we have five balls."

He looked at me funny.

The Bargain

by Sarah Schulman

WHEN EVA WAS SEVENTEEN, SHE WENT TO GET A DIAphragm. As required, she went while menstruating so that her cervix would be dilated and the object, easier to implant.

"Take out your tampax and wait for the doctor," the nurse said, exiting that emblematic cubicle the sick cannot shake and the well only recall on sight.

So she did. Fifty three minutes later, the doctor finally got to her, now a bloody adolescent mess.

"Spread your legs," he said, inserting the metal speculum. "You're crazy to be doing this, it could make you sterile. Okay, relax."

And now, forty years old, she is again waiting too long in a suffocating examining room. Pink and metallic. Her shirt is off, paper vest draped like a kleenex over an elephant. She sits on the table debating the six-month-old issue of *House Beautiful* that lies torn by the trash.

Enter Doctor, x-rays in his hand and his assistant by his side. She's an Orthodox Jew, long skirt, wig, wedding band, about nineteen.

"Hello, I'm Doctor Krasner, this is Judith."

As he hands over the films and Judith places them on the light board, Eva can see that he, also, is a religious Jew, despite the lack of head covering. He's about five years older than her, old world Judaic in the timbre of his speech. Exactly the kind of person she was brought up not to trust. All of her ancestors' litanies against the religious bolt into her consciousness. Fundamentalists. She doesn't trust him. He's religious and he's a male breast doctor.

"Okay, lie down."

"Hello, Doctor." Eva tries to lie down and shake hands at the same time. She's trying to simultaneously cooperate and assert herself. That's how it is with doctors, you have to catch their attention so that they'll do a good job. Unless you want them to ignore you altogether, which requires the same degree of cooperation but complete repression of assertion. "My name is Eva."

"My middle daughter's name is Eva. I have six daughters. Let's see what we've got here."

The examination table is pushed against the wall, which was a comfort while Eva was waiting, but now become an issue of concern. If it was in the middle of the room, he could examine both breasts by walking around the table, but since it was pushed against the wall, the doctor had to sit on it and reach over her to shift sides.

"No sons?"

"My son is a beach bum. He spends all his time at Rockaway surfing, hanging out with the girls. Weight-lifting. Your breasts are very fibrous, I can't see anything on those mammograms. Let's try the sonogram. Judith, write down *large breasts with significant markings*."

"What's a sonogram?"

Eva now had two things to think about. Something was wrong, of that she was sure. A man should not be a breast doctor, she didn't trust religious Jews, the table was in the wrong place, now she was upset by the word *large*. Plus she might have cancer. The point is that maybe this was all normal—that doesn't make it right. But maybe within the realm of a world in which men were breast doctors, this was all fine and it was her fault that she was uncomfortable. She should just worry about the cancer. She didn't like men touching her but that's what you get when you go to a clinic. Even a good, expensive one.

"I put this electricity conducting gel on this tiny machine that fits in the palm of my hand. I run the machine over the breast and then, on this video, we can see a picture of the inside of your breast. He skateboards too."

The image comes up on the monitor.

"Does your son have a tattoo?"

"No, no, no tattoo. Absolutely not. Never. I hope you don't have a tattoo."

As he moves his hand slowly on and around her breast, they can both see little cysts come in and out of focus.

"I know," Eva said, watching herself on TV. "You can't be buried in a Jewish cemetery if you have a tattoo."

"They made them have tattoos."

"I know about it."

"Look," he said, as the phone rang. "You're full of cysts. Hello."

The Doctor leaned against Eva's body, continuing the sonogram as he spoke on the phone.

"Yes, Mrs. Pollack, I'm glad you called. Yes, I'm afraid I have bad news. The tumor was malignant. You need to make an appointment for a double mastectomy."

While he was taking the doctor continued the examination, but he was slightly absent-minded now, continuing to move his hand back and forth over Eva's breast, cradling the phone receiver on his shoulder, eyes glued to the TV monitor.

"No...No...we won't know until we see the nodes. I am

telling you the truth, Mrs. Pollack. We won't know until we see the nodes. Mrs. Pollack, there is no need to count on the worst. Nowadays with radiation, chemo and medication, you may have a good chance."

Eva felt like a mouse pad. By this point, she knew that it was not her own fault that she was uncomfortable. Something was definitely not okay about the way the doctor was handling this.

"Call the surgeon and make an appointment. Who is your surgeon? He's good. Yes, I am telling you the truth. If I knew for certain that you were dying I'd tell you."

She had to get out of there. But standing up while he was sitting on her, with his hand running over her breasts and talking on the phone, just seemed to be too hard to do. She eyed her coat, calculated its distance from her arm. As soon as he hung up the phone she would make a break for it.

"Mrs. Pollack, I know that this is quite a shock." He hung up and put his newly freed hand flat down on her sternum. "Eva, we need to aspirate two cysts and do a biopsy."

"Right now?"

"Yes. A core biopsy."

"Wait," she said. "I have to call my insurance company. I need pre-approval authorization or they won't reimburse."

"What's the matter, you have bad insurance?"

"Terrible. I have to pay first and then they reimburse."

"What are you, an actress?"

"No, I'm a university professor, but I'm not full time and I have to buy my own health insurance. "

"That's terrible. Between the two mammograms and the sonogram you've already had this morning, the cost is already around $1100."

"I'll have to put it on a credit card," she said. Then she realized that she wanted the doctor to know how young she was. "I'm turning forty this year." Too young for breast cancer. She wanted him to do a good job, otherwise she could lose her tits. "My mother had cancer at 49. How old are you, doctor?"

"Forty-six. I'll tell you what," he said, looking down at her, as he was still sitting on the table leaning against her body and she was still lying, shirtless on her back. "I won't charge you for the cysts. That'll save you $500, although later you'll have to pay about $300 for the lab, but that you can put off. But I have to charge you for the biopsy."

"Thank you, doctor," she said, relieved. "That will make a big difference. It really will."

"Okay," he said, jumping off the table. "Let's aspirate those cysts before the boss comes in and charges you. Iodine."

Judith handed him a q-tip dipped in iodine.

"Okay, here we go." He dabbed the iodine on two spots on Eva's left breast. The one against the wall. "Kootchie-koo."

Oh, God, she thought.

"Look on the screen," he said. "You can see everything. Needle. These sonograms are amazing. Mammograms show nothing with large, cystic breasts like yours. Okay, here comes a little prick. Look, you can see it on the screen. Open your eyes. Eva? Eva? Look. There's the cyst and there's the needle. There it goes. Watch. Watch. I'm right inside you. Look at all that fluid. The cyst is getting smaller. Amazing. Okay, out comes the needle. There you go, Eva. Open your eyes. One more time. Here comes a little prick."

As a feminist she was upset. But as a member of the proletariat she was calculating. First of all, she might have cancer.

Otherwise, why would they do a biopsy? Being molested was bad, but not the end of the world. It happened to everyone. Bankruptcy was another matter. That could really fuck up her life. If she got up and walked out right now, she would still lose the $1100 and then the second place she went to would make her pay all over again, plus she'd have to pay the extra $500 for the aspirations that this guy wasn't charging her. And, as pathetic as it sounded, she really did not have another sixteen hundred dollars in cash or credit to cover another round of this. Even if the insurance did cover some of it, it would only be in drips and drabs that would take months to come in. That was the deal. Five hundred dollars and he got to do his routine. She just couldn't afford to leave. It would be over soon.

"Now, out comes the needle. There you go. Eva, open your eyes. See the fluid. It's yellow. That means everything's fine. If it was bloody, then we'd have to worry. What subject do you teach?"

"American Studies."

"Not math?"

"No."

"You know, Eva, now that I can see more clearly, I think you don't really need that biopsy after all."

"Really?"

"Why? You want one?"

In that case she was out of there.

"No."

She sat up.

"Good. See, I saved you money and you don't need a biopsy. I must be a good doctor."

She put on her paper vest. She didn't want to lift her breasts into her bra in front of him. The nakedness was bad enough. "I'm going to leave now."

"It was a pleasure meeting you. Let me give you my phone number. Judith will give you my home, office and the hospital. Call me anytime."

"Thank you doctor."

She wanted to vomit.

"Thank you."

He closed the door behind him and Eva took her bra down from the hook on the door.

"Excuse me, Judith? Do I pay at the front desk?"

"Yes," she said. Her sheitel was light brown, with fake bangs, cut a little too long. Of course Eva imagined her bald. "He's a nice guy, Dr. Krasner. I'm going to miss him."

"Why? Is he going to jail?" Eva slipped her arms back into her blouse.

"Excuse me?"

"Is he leaving?"

"No," Judith said. "I'm leaving. My husband and I are going to Israel for religious studies."

"All the best to you," Eva said, putting on her pumps.

"Thank you," Judith said. "Same to you."

When she got to the front desk and produced her Visa card, Eva was only a little surprised to discover that she'd been charged for the whole thing. The mammograms, the sonograms, the cysts. No discount after all. She had to pay for the whole kit and caboodle.

Failing at Latin

by Samuel Exler

I couldn't seem to get the hang of Latin—
to grab the tail end of a sentence, trapping
the slippery verb, and puzzle out agreement
locking together *ibus* and *ae* and *arum*, or remember
that quae or quod meant this or that
or who or which—a spider trap of words
that tangled me in snares of the imperfect. All this
tracked fear into my high school heart,
stalling in the thicket of a passage
where Caesar's troops put up a bridge, or camped,
or flung themselves upon the Ostrogoths;
or Cicero would cannonball poor Catiline,
bombard him with "Quae usque tandem abutere,"
thumping away while I floundered in that marsh,
sinking among the nouns and adjectives.
Zero for pride as my test marks toppled,
100% anxiety of failure, palms damp,
armpits dark with sweat; my hormones
drove my body like a tank, amo,
amas, amat, this girl or that,
of lips, to or from lips, I kiss,
you kiss, he she it kisses—How do
I get the girl to kiss? My fears sprang out
on my skin, reddened with the pimply scars

of truth, that my intellect was like a Roman version
of a Greek statue—pitted, nose gouged
out of the lustrous marble, eyes without color—
and my heart: pierced with the arrow
of the ablative absolute.

Resurrection

by Connie Sanderson

When Marcia's underwear blew
from her clothesline across the fence
to flutter into the cemetery
and onto Arthur's gravestone
he livened up enough to notice
the red silk haloing his name.

The wind tousled treetops
undulated long grasses.
Arthur wanted to wave too.
Marcia stood in a pool of light.
Wondered how to get her panties.

If Arthur could he would have risen
thrust himself between the stones
bearing high the ruby flag.
When Marcia saw him coming
she'd fling wide the iron gates, spring
through them into Arthur's arms.

Secret Dreams of Artistic Directors

by Kate Moira Ryan

(Playwright sits in a chair. ARTISTIC DIRECTOR, *played by a woman, sits in a bigger chair.)*

ARTISTIC DIRECTOR: I want..

PLAYWRIGHT: *(leans forward.)* Yes?

ARTISTIC DIRECTOR: I want...

PLAYWRIGHT: Yes?

ARTISTIC DIRECTOR: More.

PLAYWRIGHT: More?

ARTISTIC DIRECTOR: Yes. More.

PLAYWRIGHT: Okay.

ARTISTIC DIRECTOR: Great.

PLAYWRIGHT: Okay.

ARTISTIC DIRECTOR: Well?

(Playwright takes cue and stands up.)

PLAYWRIGHT: Okay. More. Great.

(Playwright backs out of the room. She stops is about to knock on the door. She stops herself. She summons the courage to knock.)

ARTISTIC DIRECTOR: Hey there.

PLAYWRIGHT: More what?

ARTISTIC DIRECTOR: More of that Ryan style.

PLAYWRIGHT: *(Repeating to herself.)* Of that Ryan style.

ARTISTIC DIRECTOR: That good old Ryan style.

PLAYWRIGHT: Okay.

ARTISTIC DIRECTOR: Okay?

PLAYWRIGHT: Okay *(Leaves. Knocks on door again.)*

ARTISTIC DIRECTOR: Hey there!

PLAYWRIGHT: Hey. After the Prozac?

ARTISTIC DIRECTOR: The Prozac?

PLAYWRIGHT: The Ryan style you mean after the Prozac?

ARTISTIC DIRECTOR: Your happy period?

PLAYWRIGHT: St. John's Wart was my happy period.

ARTISTIC DIRECTOR: Give me some of that St. John's Wart happy period Ryan Style. Not the Prozac.

PLAYWRIGHT: Not the Prozac?

ARTISTIC DIRECTOR: You weren't happy during the Prozac period.

PLAYWRIGHT: I was happy. But, I wasn't happy, happy.

ARTISTIC DIRECTOR: I want happy happy. With a little depth.

PLAYWRIGHT: Happy death?

ARTISTIC DIRECTOR: NO, DEPTH! Like Jacques Cousteau, twenty thousand leagues, LIKE GETTING THE BENDS KIND OF DEPTH.

PLAYWRIGHT: That was after St. John's Wort.

ARTISTIC DIRECTOR: NO!

PLAYWRIGHT: Yup. Depth was during the zone diet.

ARTISTIC DIRECTOR: Cabbage?

PLAYWRIGHT: Meat. Steak for breakfast, hamburger for lunch...

ARTISTIC DIRECTOR: Red meat?

PLAYWRIGHT: Yup.

ARTISTIC DIRECTOR: They still make red meat?

PLAYWRIGHT: Yup. I was happy, happy focused with depth.

ARTISTIC DIRECTOR: That's what I want. Happy, happy focused with depth.

PLAYWRIGHT: Okay.

ARTISTIC DIRECTOR: Okay?

PLAYWRIGHT: Great.

ARTISTIC DIRECTOR: See you.

PLAYWRIGHT: Going off to rewrite my happy, happy focused with depth play.

ARTISTIC DIRECTOR: Oh, I almost forgot kill that girl.

PLAYWRIGHT: The girl?

ARTISTIC DIRECTOR: I think you should kill her. Get rid of her.

PLAYWRIGHT: Kill her?

ARTISTIC DIRECTOR: The girl. Kill her. But, make it happy, happy focused with depth.

PLAYWRIGHT: Okay, she's dead.

ARTISTIC DIRECTOR: Don't want to even see her on stage. Kill her like you killed the other five characters. They weren't... *(Pause.)* What's that word?

PLAYWRIGHT: Necessary?

ARTISTIC DIRECTOR: No. That word, what's that word.

PLAYWRIGHT: Interesting?

ARTISTIC DIRECTOR: No. That word.

PLAYWRIGHT: Likeable?

ARTISTIC DIRECTOR: Yes. Exactly. So kill her. She's not likeable. Make it only...

PLAYWRIGHT: Happy, happy focused characters now with depth who are likeable.

ARTISTIC DIRECTOR: Exactly. Thanks for coming by.

PLAYWRIGHT: Right. And thank you. Great notes.

ARTISTIC DIRECTOR: Thanks for coming by.

(Walks her to the door. She opens the door. The playwright walks out. The artistic director shuts the door and locks it. Playwright turns around frantic.)

PLAYWRIGHT: Wait a second. I can't kill the girl. *(Tries to open the door. It is locked.)*

SHE'S THE ONLY CHARACTER LEFT!

(The playwright starts pounding on the door. The artistic director has a wide grin on her face. She begins to cackle madly.)

FastFreddyDumas

by Ryan Land

I'm on the #55 and he's two benches behind, spinning his tales. Grand gestures and glory days. If he doesn't keep his legend alive, no one will. He's the keeper of self. The great weaver. His hair is tall and Elvisesque. His garb is grandiose, as is his personality. This trickster wears faux-skin boots with shiny buckles that jingle when he pours up and out of his seat. With a worldly gait he clops toward the fold-open doors. For him, this is the grand ballroom entrance to a world of possibility. As he begins to step down(and out), he hesitates for an instant and turns to his audience in the back of the bus.

"Freddy. Fast Freddy Dumas."

It rolled confidently off his tongue. Candy for my ear.

from Señoritas in Love

by Jaime Manrique

Those who try to come near it are insane
and those who reach it are shaken by grief.

ANNA AKHMATOVA
(trans. by Jane Kenyon with Vera Dunham)

I
THE WILLA CATHER OF BANK STREET

This season, five years after Ramón's death, his face has been conspicuous all over town, appearing in many newspapers and magazines. With the posthumous publication of his autobiography, Ramón has finally made it and even those who despised him while he was alive have to acknowledge him now.

Nowadays I live on Bank Street in Greenwich Village. But the other night, feeling nostalgic for those days when I met Ramón and we became lovers, I went back to visit my old Times Square neighborhood.

Walking down 42nd to 8th Avenue, I noticed that the most notorious sex joints had been closed, that there were more cops than criminals on the street. I ambled along 8th Avenue in the direction of O'Donells bar which—in typical gentrification manner—had been renamed O'Donnell's Camp.

This was the year, too, when the old Times Square had finally closed down; when the fashion police, wearing Donna Karan uniforms, had been replaced by cops in Mickey Mouse hats, the year when 42nd Street—that erstwhile Grand Canyon of seediness— had become a Disney amusement park, metamorphosing the old sleazy grotesquerie into a soulless mall. Yet the main difference between then and the present was that back then I thought of myself as young and light-hearted; back then I had already experienced sadness and disappointments, but my life had not been touched by tragedy.

I'm getting ahead of myself. The story I want to tell begins shortly after I published my Christopher Columbus epic poem and I still lived above O'Donnell's bar. When the tome was published, the only essential missing from my life was love. Like every single person on the isle of Manhattan between the ages of 8 and 80, I became seriously interested in finding a mate. I had turned thirty-five the year I became a published author, and a middle-aged gay man has fewer chances of finding a boyfriend than a Washington politician has of entering the kingdom of heaven.

Despite the lack of romance, I was happy at last. With the publication of my epic poem, life in Times Square seemed rosier than ever. Yet, try as hard as I could, I couldn't get away from the subject of love because all my single friends, and even my septuagenarian mother, were desperately looking for their other half.

I tried to pretend that I was above all that. When Mother called to complain about the lack of appropriate, and available, men in Jackson Heights, or on the Scandinavian cruises she patronized, I'd say, "Mother, remember you're not American. You are Colombian, and love is not at the top of the Colombian agenda."

Happiness is fleeting, as we all know. One day my sainted landlady died of a heart attack; her greedy children took over the management of the building, and tripled my rent. I took the money I had received from a grant given by the Colombian Civic Center in Jackson Heights (it was rumored the money was put up by the Cali cartel to launder dollars into this country—though my mother vehemently denied it). "People who live in glass houses, Santiago," she said, "shouldn't look inside the horse's mouth." I knew what she meant so I decided to move to a less hectic neighborhood than Hell's Kitchen, one more befitting an aging homosexual.

That's how I came to move to Bank Street. I fancied Bank Street for two reasons: the American author Willa Cather had lived very productively at 5 Bank Street for almost two decades. And I liked looking out of my window and feeling that I lived in what looked like a set for a Merchant/Ivory production. Instead of hookers and junkies, I saw mainly neurotic gay men, walking their neurotic little dogs. The unpleasant aspect of an otherwise enchanting street was the neighborhood psychopathic homophobe who walked his huge doberman without a leash, taunting homosexuals. Another annoying part of living on Bank (which is as white a street as exists in Manhattan) was that often, on my way home, or as I exited the building, some little old lady would come sprinting after me and asked me questions like, "Mr. Super, where do I put the newspapers?" Other times, some arriviste, and unctuous yuppie, would approach me with a hand in his pocket and say, "Excuse me, Super, if you can help me get an apartment on Bank I could make it worth your while." Racism aside, the loveliness of the street was quite soothing. It was, I knew, a great place for me to become the professional writer I'd always wanted to be.

My apartment was on the second floor of a three-story townhouse. My friend Manolo, who helped me move into my new digs, had warned me, "Watch out, Santiago, the nicer the building, the meaner the people."

Fall arrived and, for the first time in my years in Manhattan, I was fully aware of it as a real season because there were actually trees on Bank Street. As soon as the weather cooled, I began using the fireplace in my living room and spending my evenings at home reading. Boyfriend or not, I was determined to enjoy my life. Besides, since I had enough savings to last me several months (if I was careful with my money) I decided I'd start another epic poem, this one about pre-Columbian life on the savannah of Bogotá. For years, I had been reading about the Chibcha culture that inhabited the savannah and I found myself often daydreaming, trying to reconstruct their world. Before I got started, I thought it would be a good idea to give Tim Colby, my agent, a call.

I hesitated before calling him. Last year, after twenty-five years in the business, one of Tim's authors had become a huge best-seller in the United States and all over the world. It turns out that his Salvadorean cleaning lady, Juanita Chuchimurringi, who had been cleaning Tim's office for over a decade, had been taking home and reading all the books Tim agented. She had written an autobiography spanning her seventy years, beginning with her life in the jungles of El Salvador to her trek on foot to the United States. The book, each chapter written in the manner of a famous Latin American author, had been hailed as one of the most avant garde autobiographies ever written. I was jealous, very jealous. To make matters worse, the old Tim Colby I knew—the man who brought me bagels with cream cheese when he came by to see me and to talk about great books—had suddenly turned big-shot agent. I decided to make the call anyway and inform Tim of my plans.

"Before you get started," he said, "let's get together for lunch. How about tomorrow at one?" Tim gave me the name of a Chinese restaurant near Cooper Union.

Tim had been after me to write a thriller about Colombia. A literary thriller, of course. He had tried to hook me up with an important editor at a major house. For a while I wandered about the city looking at every situation to see if it had the potential to be turned into a thriller. But finally I came to the conclusion that I had no access to the worlds in which thrilling things took place. In the days when I had been an interpreter, I had worked one afternoon for a Peruvian middle-aged roly-poly man who asked me to accompany him to places all over town where he bought literature about explosives. But even if he had been a member of the now defunct Shining Path, what did I know about that stuff? God knows lots of thriller-like things took place in Jackson Heights, but for the sake of making some bucks I wasn't willing to run the risk of going underground, getting a new identity as well as total reconstructive plastic surgery. I had met a man who had done that, and he looked like a plastic Disney creature broiled in a microwave. I decided I simply did not have what it took to write a thriller, literary or not, and Tim was disappointed when I shot down the idea for good.

I hadn't seen Tim in months. Since he was not known for his punctuality, I meandered on my way to the restaurant. Tim was usually between a half hour to two hours late. In this respect, he was the perfect agent for a Colombian author: Tim lived on

Colombian time. But when I arrived at the restaurant five minutes late, Tim was not only there (this was the first sign of how corporate he had become) but he was also sporting an Armani jacket and tie. It took me awhile to get used to Tim's new look. For many years he had supplemented his agenting working as a messenger on Wall Street, but now he looked like a banker.

We ordered lunch. As we ate, Tim entertained me with stories about Juanita Chuchimurringi, the author who had made him a millionaire. One story was about how the day he had given Juanita a check for a million dollars, in the same restaurant, for the sale of her paperback edition, Juanita had fainted. "Can you imagine, Santiago," Tim laughed, "I wanted to give her a nice surprise, but instead I almost killed her. She is seventy-five years old now."

I was sick of hearing about Juanita Chuchimurringi. I knew very well he found anything she did charming. He had to—she had made him a millionaire. His only complaint was that he had not been able to find another cleaning lady who did as thorough a job, though Juanita had offered to continue doing it. But he was my agent too, though now I seemed to have become merely a friend to whom he could brag about his star's innumerable triumphs: meeting Brad Pitt, appearing on Oprah, being invited by García Márquez to teach in his journalism school in Barranquilla, receiving a nobility title from the Kings of Spain.

Tim sipped his wine. "Look, Santiago. Her success is good for you, too. It means that, as your agent, I have a lot of clout. I can get you a really good deal now. What happened for her, I can make happen for you."

I was ashamed of my envy, but more than anything else, I was ashamed of revealing myself as another jealous author, mortified by someone else's good fortune. It could be, too, that since Juanita had gone through the roof, my relationship with Tim had changed. I missed the old days when we'd get together to dream of great accomplishments. What irked me, I suppose, is that his turn had come whereas I was still completely unknown outside of the circle of my mother's "literary" girlfriends in Jackson Heights.

"There's somebody I want you to meet. I think the two of you would be a great match. Her name's Carola Terry and she's very interested in Latin American writing."

I must have looked unimpressed because Tim said, "And she doesn't want you to write a thriller. She's looking for young new novelists she can launch."

"But I was thinking of writing another epic poem."

Tim put down his fork. He looked at me with a focus I had never seen in him before. "Santiago, look, you're not a kid anymore. The only reason I can afford to keep you as a client is because of Juanita's success."

I squirmed on my seat and swallowed a large chunk of spicy tofu. Could he utter one sentence, I wondered, without mentioning Her name?

"Let me put it this way, how many copies did you sell of 'Christopher Columbus on his Deathbed'?"

"I don't know," I said, although I knew quite well.

Tim stared at me, and with one hand motioned the waiter to approach the table. "Check," he said.

"Okay, 380 copies." Three hundred of which had been purchased by my mother to give to her friends in Jackson Heights, to the people in the soup kitchen where she did volunteer work one night a week, and the remainder for our relatives in Colombia.

"I rest my case," Tim said, as he took the bill and deposited a crisp hundred-dollar note on the plate. "Look, I have to go now. I have to meet with the people at Paramount. They want to make Juanita's next three books into movies."

"She's written three more books?" I asked, stunned.

"Of course not. But that's how you do it nowadays—I don't sell a book unless there's a movie attached to it. They'll make the movies from her outlines as she's writing her memoirs."

I sighed. Tim must really like me, I thought. Otherwise, why would he bother with me. He's running on a track too fast for me.

"Look, on my way to the meeting, I'm going to call Carola Terry," he said pulling his cellular out of his breast pocket. "I'm sure we can arrange a meeting in the next twenty-four hours. We've got to strike while the iron is hot. But be ready for that meeting, *amigo*. I know you can rise to the occasion. By the way," he said, as he rose from his chair, "make sure you cast the book before you come to the meeting."

"Cast it? I don't even know what the book is all about yet."

"It doesn't matter, Santiago. This is book biz in the new millennium. Just make sure you get bankable stars—I've got all the connections. When I call from this phone," he said, shaking his cellular, "Disney answers. I'll call you later today. So be there or be square. Think big names. By the way, the change is yours," he concluded, referring to what was left of the $100. "Live a little while I go out there to make you rich and famous."

I walked home. I was too disturbed to sit in a taxi. I knew that success made people crazy, but I didn't know that entirely new personalities could emerge. I had barely made it through the door of my apartment when the phone rang. "Santiago, what's up?" Tim said. "We're meeting tomorrow at Carola's office. Ten o'clock sharp. Don't be a minute late. Remember, the cast is everything. *Ciao*, baby. By tomorrow at this time, I hope to have made you a millionaire."

I spent the rest of the day obsessing about the meeting. I couldn't think of a novel I was ready to write yet and I certainly couldn't cast it before knowing what it was about. I decided the best thing to do was to go to bed early, get a good night's sleep, and wake up early and perky for my important meeting.

As I was getting ready for bed, I heard what sounded like my downstairs neighbor yelling, "Get in that closet, you dirty dog." This was followed by a door slamming shut, and my neighbor's voice bellowing, "Stay there til morning. You're punished for the night." My neighbor was a young, attractive blonde living on the ground floor, whom I often saw going in and out of the premises in a lavender spandex jogging outfit. I hadn't realized that she had a pet. Still, whatever the dog had done, the punishment sounded excessive. Thinking no more of it I went to sleep, but awoke at dawn, too wired about my meeting to be able to sleep. I found myself listening for the noises coming from downstairs to see if I could hear any barking or yelping. Getting along with my neighbors has always been one of my mottos, but if this woman was torturing her pet, I would have to report her to the authorities.

By eight o'clock, after several cups of coffee and a hot shower, I was ready for my meeting. As absurd as the whole thing sounded, I wondered whether this was going to be the turning point in my life as a novelist.

The publisher's swank offices were located in midtown, right in the middle of the theatre district. My Christopher Columbus book had been published by Spirit of the Underdog Press, a one-man operation run by a Colombian friend of mine in Jackson

Heights. This publisher was definitely a step up for me. When I arrived at the 28th floor, I noticed the walls were decorated with bookjackets of many authors I recognized, along with show biz types and corrupt politicians. A young assistant came out promptly to greet me leading me to the office of Carola Terry, where Tim was already seated on a comfortable chair, sipping a cup of cappuccino.

Carola Terry's office overlooked The Great White Way. She sat behind an imposing desk. Carola was a still young, attractive woman dressed in a well-cut suit that screamed money and power. She was smallish, slender and her blond hair was cut short. Her alert blue eyes were precision tools used for appraising anything that came in their path. As she shook my hand with her firm grip, and looked me up and down, I felt as though she was totalling my whole worth. At that moment I was hoping I passed her test as a potential money object. Santiago, I thought, you'd better get your act together in the next five seconds.

We chit-chatted pleasantly for a couple of minutes, and just when I was beginning to relax, she said, "Tim tells me that you're writing a romantic novel set in Latin America, about three powerful women. I take it the book is set against a glamorous background of corruption and drugs. I tell you, Santiago. You know the success we had with Juanita Chuchimurringi, and, to be quite frank with you, I'd like to find her male counterpart. A man who can write well about women. A man with a muscular, yet seductive, voice."

I smiled at her while thinking of what to say. When nothing came to mind I looked in Tim's direction.

"Tell Carola who you have cast for the roles...the three actresses we discussed."

I did a double take. What if I said the wrong thing?

"Go ahead, the two young actresses we agreed upon," Tim said. "The older one we haven't really decided on."

"I can't wait!" Carola salivated, now looking at me as if I had turned into a mountain of gold.

"Well...Winona Ryder," I ventured, to see what reaction I'd get.

There was no reaction from Carola or Tim.

"And then...Gwyneth Paltrow," I added, though I detested her; but she seemed to be in every recent movie I saw.

"And, well, you know...," I intoned as slowly as I could, hoping to be rescued by one of them.

"I've got it!" Carola said, jumping up from her chair. "For the older woman, Michelle Pfeiffer. Oh what a brilliant cast—though it may be a little too close to 'The Age of Innocence.' And we may have to change Winona Ryder for a Latino actor, you know. Perhaps Jennifer Lopez? We do have to take these things into consideration—although, don't get me wrong, I am not politically correct. Now we need the male lead. Someone sexy and hot at the box office."

"Antonio Banderas," I offered.

"That's perfect," Carola Terry exulted walking to her window and looking down at Broadway. "I see it already," she said, pointing down to the Great White Way. "In big letters...." She was casting about for a title but was having trouble finding one.

"How about...One Hundred Years of Spirits?" I offered.

"Oh you're wicked, Santiago," Tim said, blushing.

"I like that," said Carola. "I like my writers to have a sense of humor. But seriously. We need an evocative title. Something grand like 'Gone with the Wind.' Something rich..."

"How about Rich Ladies of the Andes?" I said.

Tim got up from his sofa. "Of course," he said pointing to me, "we want to retain all movie, CD-ROM, foreign and paperback rights."

Carola paced slowly back to her desk, sat down and said, "We'll discuss all that tomorrow at lunch, Tim, you and I. We don't want to burden the author with all these details. We want Santiago to worry about nothing except his creative decisions."

Tim sat down, so it was my turn to get up; I walked over to the window. Broadway was hopping. It wasn't too long ago that I had been like one of those people down there, often passing this building and totally oblivious to what went on here.

"Santiago," Carola said, bringing me back to reality. "Is two okay with you?"

"Three," Tim came back quickly.

"Three...novels?" I asked

"No, I can only sign you up for one."

"She's offering you three hundred thousand dollars," Tim said, as if we were talking about ice-cream scoops. "Though I personally think that idea is worth three million. You're lucky you're getting it for practically nothing, Carola. The next one will be three million. You mark my words."

"The sky's the limit," Carola enthused, "if this one works out. Now, Santiago," she turned and gave me a hard look. "Remember what I want. Something big, romantic. Something with a lot of scope. Preferably with lots of magic realism, which is what people like. Can you write it in six months? 400 pages? It will be one of our big books for the spring season, year after next. I'll get our lawyers to write the contract and it'll be ready in couple of weeks and...."

"Santiago wants most of it upfront," Tim said, getting up again, a fighting cock ready to draw blood.

Carola stood too, her chest full-blown, her hands splayed on her hips. "We'll talk about that at lunch." Then she turned to me. "I'm going to call Peter Weir this afternoon and run it by him. He could do a great job. I've been longing for a movie like 'The Year of Living Dangerously' for a long time. Is Peter Weir okay with you?"

"Oh sure," I said. "Since we can't bring D.W. Griffith back, Peter Weir will have to do."

Downstairs, outside the building, Tim turned to embrace me and kissed me on both cheeks. "You're a great negotiator," he said. "Watch out, Santiago. I'm going to make you as rich and famous as Juanita Chuchimurringi. We won't stop until you're a count of Spain."

At that moment I felt like saying, "Tim, I'll give you the whole three hundred thousand if you promise never to mention Juanita's name to me again."

"I gotta go meet Madonna," Tim said. "I can't be late. Maybe I'll put her in touch with you. You like the idea?"

"How about Madonna for the older woman in the movie?" I suggested.

Tim shook his head. "No, Michelle Pfeiffer, Sigourney Weaver. We need older actresses for that role." Then he hailed a taxi and left me there on Broadway and 45th, $300,000 richer. I decided I'd walk home. I needed to exhaust myself to calm the thoughts racing in my brain.

2
9000 YEARS AGO

For the next couple of days, looking for ways to distract myself until I found out whether the deal had been finalized, I decided to investigate about my downstairs neighbor a little more. But as hard as I tried, I never saw her walking a dog, nor did I hear any animal noises coming from her apartment. I did notice that she went jogging around noon each day, regardless of the weather. I decided that she must have been keeping care of a pet for a friend who was away and had returned it to the owner. Now and then, however, my Colombian imagination got the best of me and it crossed my mind that in a rage my neighbor might have killed her pet and stored it in her closet, or her fridge. Just to make sure, whenever I passed her front door, I'd pause ever so slightly taking a deep whiff to try to detect the rotting pet. The only thing I noticed was that just about every night, around the time I was getting ready for bed, her bell would ring.

And then, as I was about to start obsessing about the mysterious young woman, Tim called. The deal had gone through. He apologized for not being able to get me more than three, but he said he hoped I'd be happy with the deal; he assured me that next time he would get me seven. "Seven hundred thousand?" I asked. "No, no, Santiago. Seven figures. And I'm not talking any seven figures." It would be a few weeks before the contract would be ready for signing and the check would follow soon after. "If you need some dough to tide you over, just yell," he said. "I'd be happy to advance you whatever you need." Overcoming my astonishment, I thanked him for everything he had done for me, promised I'd deliver a knockout manuscript, and reassured him that I still had some money left from my grant. "So, then just go for it, Santiago. Don't wait for the contract or the check. Let's get this book done within the year. I have big plans for you. Next year, by now, I want you living next door to us in Connecticut. There's a great place I know where you can get fabulous horses. I want people to start calling you Don Santiago. From now on, every two years, I want a Santiago Martinez novel out there, outselling Stephen King."

When he hung up I realized that, for the first time in a year, Tim hadn't mentioned Juanita Chuchimurringi, not even once. I was so grateful to him for this that I decided not to disappoint him and to begin my novel the next day. But what, exactly, was I going to write about? I knew that it would take place in Colombia, that there were three main women characters and at least one major male romantic figure. I also knew that Carola wanted politics, revolution, glamour, and romance. Did this mean that I was selling out? Would writing something like this kill my poetic soul? I punched my friend Herbert's digits. I told him about what had happened and that now I was concerned about whether I would ever be able to take myself seriously again. Herbert was in his sixties, a trust lawyer who lived on Park Avenue. We had met one day at the Film Forum, watching a horrendous avant garde film that consisted of the screen turning red, redder, reddest. At one point, unable to contain myself, I uttered, "This is too boring for words." "Pretentious piece of crap," said the man sitting next to me. I got up to leave and Herbert followed me. Outside the theatre, bonded by our hatred of the movie we had seen, we started a conversation and struck a up friendship that centered mainly around going to the movies once a month. Whenever I was in a quandary, I would go to Herbert for advice.

He seemed to be the soul of practicality, and was the only successful American I knew. My mother's friends in Jackson Heights were richer, but at least Herbert had made his money without breaking the law.

"Will people ever accept me again as a good writer?" I asked, tormented by this doubt.

"What people?" he said. "Nobody knows who you are, so forget about that. And what do you want with 'good,' Santiago? In this country, if you have money you're good. Half of those people out there who've made it were born with a diamond rattler in their hands. Listen to me, if you make lots of money, if you're a success, you'll immediately become 'good.' That, trust me, is the American way. So, don't even think twice about it. Anyhow, it doesn't sound like they asked you to write crap. A poetic 'Gone with the Wind,' that's what you have to think about. I've got to go, but there are a bunch of new movies I haven't seen so call me next week and we'll make plans."

"It's settled, then," I thought. "When my grant money runs out I don't want to go back to interpreting. I want to be a writer. To stay home and write."

Now that I had a deal, I called mother to tell her the news. When I finished explaining about the novel I was going to write, the movie, the advance, I distinctly got the impression she didn't believe a word I had said. So I decided to go visit her in Queens and try to explain in person what had happened and how my life had changed.

"Come right over," she said. "I made the most delicious *mondongo,* and I made so much I was just going to take the left- overs to my Church."

A big steaming bowl of tripe soup with *picante* sounded like what the doctor had ordered. I grabbed my coat and left for Times Square, to transfer there to the Number 7 train. I never went to my mother's hoping to be comforted, or understood. Just as ostriches stick their heads in the sand to escape from reality, I went to visit Mom because once there, my life in Manhattan seemed so far away that I could put everything on hold. Visiting her in Jackson Heights was like taking a trip to another galaxy that offered different kinds of life forms than the ones I am accustomed to.

My mother was living alone once more. My sister Wilbrajan had moved to Miami, where she had a thriving singing career, and she had taken her son Gene with her. All the reports we got from them were that they were happy and had no intentions of returning for a long while, though with Wilbrajan one never knew. Mother, who never ceased to surprise me, had turned over a new leaf. She didn't seem to miss Gene at all. She had taken to travelling alone or with the Urrutias, and recently had returned from a pilgrimage to the Holy Land. Although she had always been interested in spirituality (meaning *santería*), lately she had become extremely active in her Church, becoming a member of many committees, going on retreats, and cooking huge *sancochos* for their soup kitchen. The other, and most remarkable, change in her life was her interest in the commodities market, where she was making piles of money. It all had started when Paulina Urrutia had given Mother a computer for her birthday. Since Paulina and Claudia were always travelling (running from the DEA was more like it), she was on the Internet. Now that they both had computers, they could E-mail each other every day, no matter where Paulina was. And then, maybe because Paulina was such a whiz making money, Mother started playing the commodities market.

When I let myself in through the door, Mother was in the living room, temporarily away from her terminal, reading *Business Investors' News*. She had a towel wrapped around her neck, to protect herself from Simón Bolívar's shit. The hideous parrot was perched on her shoulders.

"Hi, Sammy," she said, in her usual cheerful manner. "You look like you haven't had a good meal in days. Go to the kitchen and pop the *mondongo* in the microwave. Three minutes. And I just made some cheese *arepas* for you."

I was more than happy to leave her alone with Simón Bolívar, who, as soon as he saw me, started squawking. I was finishing a delicious bowl of soup, with the scrumptious *arepas,* when mother came into the room, startling me.

"Please sit across the table, I don't want that bird shitting on my food," I demanded.

"You're such a baby, Sammy. You're just jealous of him. A grown up man jealous of a parrot! Who ever heard of such a thing?"

To my relief, she put the bird on his perch, but she kept the shit spattered towel draped over her shoulders.

"And to what do I owe the honor of your visit? I thought I only heard from you when you need a loan, but apparently you have plenty of money now."

Why *had* I come to visit? Why did I think this time around she would understand me any better than before?

"I wanted to see you. I thought it would make you happy that I'm a success," I said, knowing how important money was in her eyes, and how she saw me as a failure because I hadn't made lots of it.

"Well, I hope you've made plans to invest that money," she said, seeming to concede that my deal was not a product of wishful thinking. "You know, the thing about money is that you need to keep making it all the time. If you don't, you run out of it. Have you decided how to invest it yet?"

I shook my head.

"Santiago, you don't seem happy. Something's bothering you. You seem as lost as ever. Oh, I see… you're having trouble writing your book? See, I told you. You should move back to Queens. This is where your roots are. What are you doing living with those Wasps? Is that what you want to be—one of God's frozen people? How do you expect to write about this place if you are a stranger to your constituents?"

"Who said I am not happy? And who said I'm blocked writing my book? And anyway…constituents. Where do you get such words? I'm a writer, not a politician. For God's sake, stop trying to make me feel like a traitor to Jackson Heights. In any case, it has nothing to do with my writing either; my writing's going fine," I boasted, lying through my teeth since I hadn't written the first line of my book yet.

"Hum… I think you need to see Matilde."

"What for? There's nothing wrong with me! No way I'm gonna go consult any witches."

"She'd be really hurt if she heard you calling her that. She likes you a lot, Santiago. Besides, I don't know how many times I have to tell you she's not a witch. She's an intuitive consultant."

"That's some fancy pc name for Voodoo," I snorted. "I really don't want any chickens sacrificed in my name. Thanks, anyway."

"Well then since you're here, would you like to learn how to multiplicate your money? Because knowing you, if you do get that money, it wouldn't surprise me if you go through it in no time. I'm gonna show you how to make your money grow."

"If you mean the commodities exchange, no thanks. I have other faults, but I'm not a gambler."

"May I remind you that I've made more money in the last year than in all the other years of my life put together. You should at least be happy. When I'm gone all that money will go to you and your sister and Gene. You know, what if you get writer's block and you're not able to write your novel? You'll have to return all that money. I'm not going to bail you out."

"I wouldn't expect you to, Mother."

"Anyway, I think you should let me teach you a few things. You know, I may not be around much longer to teach you everything like you like you are still in kindergarten."

"Wait a minute—what are you trying to say? Is there anything wrong with you? Do you have any health problems I don't know about?"

"Do I look sick to you, Santiago?" she said, sitting up straight, her chin thrust out, her shoulders back, her surgery enhanced bust sticking out.

The truth was she looked great. Stunning. Of course she'd always be a beautiful woman even if she lived to be 100 years old. But what made her attractive was not her physical gifts—which were considerable — but something, some strength, a kind of power—that she radiated from within. "I've never felt better in my life."

Could she be hinting about moving back to Colombia, as she threatened every so often? Something *was* up then. But what? Whatever it was, she was not about to let me in on it.

Getting up from her chair, she announced, "Come and see

how I do it." Whereupon she walked to Simón Bolívar's perch, installed the bird on her shoulder and left the room.

I had no choice but to go into her office where her terminal was set up, complete with state-of-the-art software. The screen was flashing the latest stock market quotations as Mother sat at her chair, put on her glasses and waited. I stood behind her.

Suddenly, the parrot squawked and Mother picked up her pencil and scribbled something on a note pad. "Yes, we'll buy a ton of cotton," she said.

"You mean to tell me that you buy every time that bird screeches?"

"And why not? He's made me the richest woman in Jackson Heights. I mean, the richest *honest* woman in Jackson Heights."

"But don't you realize that bird squawks every thirty seconds? It's just a nervous reflex!"

"The hell it is."

"Just watch," I said. "I'll time it and maybe this will convince you."

Both mother and the parrot stared at me as I held my watch inches from my nose. Thirty seconds passed, thirty-five, fifty, a minute went buy and still the damned bird remained silent. I looked up—humiliated—and saw mother's gloating smile.

"By the way, before I forget, Carmen Elvira asked me to ask you to read for the Christmas Benefit at the Colombian Civic Center. And I want you to know that Colombia's Beauty Queen has already accepted. They're trying to get the soccer team. Can you imagine, you on the stage, with all those luminaries? I'd be so proud of you. This is a moment of real effervescence in the Colombian community. That soccer team of ours has really unified Jackson Heights."

Just to spite her, I added, "Sure—was put together with the Cali cartel's money. Besides, I'm not giving readings these days."

"You can read from 'Christopher Columbus,'" she said, not willing to concede defeat. "You know, I've never been able to read the whole thing."

Her philistinism was more than I could bear. "I don't want to hear Christopher Columbus' name again for the rest of my life," I snapped back. "I'm sick of it."

"You wrote it, I didn't. Or you can read from your novel, if you have anything written, that is. But you cannot, I repeat can-*not*, decline. This is a benefit for the Colombian Civic Center, Santiago. I have to think of the family's name. After all, I'm the one who lives here."

"The Civic Center indeed," I ranted. "It should be called the Cynic Center because it's full of people laundering drug money while they pretend to care about culture."

"Squawk," went Simón Bolívar.

"What? What?" said mother, turning to face the screen. "Oh. Bananas. Of course we'll buy bananas, darling."

Contributors

STEPHEN CRAMER has most recently published work in *High Plains Literary Review* and *Brilliant Corners: A Journal of Jazz and Literature.* He lives in New York City.

ROBERT DANBERG lives in New York City with his wife Mary Biggs and son, Rubin Danberg-Biggs. His poems have appeared in *Ploughshares* and *Kerem*.

MEGHAN DAUM'S essays and articles have appeared in *The New Yorker*, *The New York Times Book Review*, *GQ*, and *Self*, among other publications. She lives in New York City.

KRISTIN ELIASBERG writes on culture and the arts for *The Nation*, *The New Yorker* (listings section), *The Village Voice*, *Book-Forum*, and other publications. She is currently on a Knight Fellowship for Journalists at the Yale Law School and also works as a professional modern dancer and choreographer. She is currently working on a collection of stories/essays not unlike the one featured in this issue.

EVE ENSLER'S bio appears on page 87.

SAMUEL EXLER is the author of *Ambition, Fertility, Loneliness,* of which Robert Bly has written, "I am often moved by the grieving weight...of these poems." His poems have appeared in a number of anthologies, and in many literary journals, including *New York Quarterly, Poetry East,* and *Plainsong*. He has been a print production manager, combat infantry soldier, warehouse worker, advertising copywriter, and psychotherapist. A graduate of Brooklyn College, where he was editor-in-chief of the student magazine, he now lives in Philadelphia.

SCOTT FERGUSON is a poet who lives in New York City. He has an MFA from Columbia University and his work has been published in such journals as *The Iowa Review,* the *Brooklyn Review,* and *American Letters Commentary.* He is currently at work on a collection of poetry and prose.

CAROLYN FERRELL is the author of *Don't Erase Me: Stories.* Her short stroy "Proper Library" was selected by John Updike for inclusion in *The Best American Short Stories of the Century.* She lives in New York City.

STAN FRIEDMAN has had a long and obscure career as a poet and hack writer. For instance, he currently pens cookbook reviews for *Publishers Weekly*, and his poetry can be found in the next issue of *Pittsburgh Quarterly*. He is keeping his day job as Senior Librarian for Condé Nast Publications. With an MFA from Columbia and a degree in Library Science from Rutgers, Stan not only awaits publishing his first book, he knows just where he will shelve it.

DANIEL KANE has poems published or forthcoming in *The Denver Quarterly*, *Exquisite Corpse, Gargoyle*, *Hanging Loose*, and other journals.

WAYNE KOESTENBAUM'S third book of poetry, *The Milk of Inquiry,* is published in Spring 1999 by Persea. He is a professor of English at the Graduate Center of the City University of New York.

RYAN LAND recently graduated from the Bachelor of Education program at the University of Winnipeg. He majored in English and minored in Physical Education. He breathes teaching, learning, reading, writing, his partner (Carmilla), and his first child (Cohen), in equal parts.

JANICE LEVY is the 1998 First Place Winner in the Writer's Digest Literary Short Story Contest.

JAIME MANRIQUE is a novelist, poet, and essayist. His most recent books are *My Night with Federico Garcia Lorca* (poetry) 1995, and the novels *Latin Moon in Manhattan* (1992) and *Twilight at the Equator* (1997). His autobiography, *Eminent Maricones: Arenas, Lorca, Puig, and Me* was published in July, 1999.

REBECCA McCLANAHAN is the author of five books, most recently *Word Painting: A Guide to Writing More Descriptively* (Writer's Digest Books) and poems, essays, and stories in *The Georgia Review, The Gettysburg Review, Southern Review, Kenyon Review, Boulevard, Seventeen,* and numerous literary magazines throughout the country. She has received a Pushcart Prize in fiction, the Wood Prize from *Poetry* magazine, and the Carter prize for the essay from *Shenandoah.* Her work appears in *The Best American Poetry 1998;* it has also been twice listed as "notable" in *The Best American Essays,* and has been aired on NPR's "The Sound of Writing." She lives in New York City.

JOHNNIE MORELLO is a writer, performer, and theatre director. *He Looked at Me Funny* was initially included in his one-man performance of *SOME noBODIES,* staged in Chicago. His play *Hacking New York* received a *DRAMA-logue* award for its Hollywood production. He currently lives and works in Los Angeles.

BETSEY OSBORNE is a contributing editor at *Vanity Fair.* She has also worked at other magazines including *The New Yorker, Grand Street, Columbia: A Magazine of Poetry and Prose,* and the *Brooklyn Review.* Born in Auburn, N.Y., she lives in New York City.

GRACE PALEY'S most recent book, *Just As I Thought,* is a collection of essays, reviews and lectures. Her *Collected Short Stories* was published in 1994.

GERRY GOMEZ PEARLBERG is the author of *Marianne Faithfull's Cigarette* (Cleis), a 1999 Lambda Book Award finalist. She also edited *Queer Dog* (Cleis), winner of a '98 Firecracker Alternative Book Award. She teaches poetry at The Writer's Voice in NYC.

DIANE RAINTREE, a screenwriter who played a talking dog in a rightfully obscure indie flick and appeared in a spoof infomercial on Comedy Central, loves early mornings and late nights in her big backyard in Chelsea, hitting occasionally splendid shots on pitch and putt golf courses, and driving around her home state, Vermont, in the summer.

MEGAN RATNER has contributed non-fiction to the *New York Times, Art/Text,* and *Filmmaker.*

KATE MOIRA RYAN won the Young Playwrights Festival Award in 1985, and received her MFA from Columbia University in 1990. She has grants and fellowships from NYFA, New Dramatists, a Van Lier Fellowship from The Women's Project, Yaddo, McDowell, the Edward Albee and Helene Wurlitzer Foundations and the Brooks Atkinson Fellowship to London's Royal National Theater. She is a recent winner of New Dramatists, Joe A. Callaway Award. She has been commissioned by *Rent* director Michael Greif to adapt Dorothy Allison's *Cavedweller* for the stage. Recent productions include *The Worgelt Study* at Dixon Place and *Damage and Desire* at Baliwick Rep in Chicago.

CONNIE SANDERSON is a former high school teacher, who divides her time between Decorah, IA and Lynxville, WI. Her poetry has appeared in *Yankee*, *Wisconsin Review*, *Lyrical Iowa*, *frogpond*, *100 Words*, and *The Spoon River Poetry Review*. She is currently compiling a book of poems in collaboration with her sister.

SARAH SCHULMAN'S most recent books are *Shimmer* (Avon, 1998) a novel about the Red Scare and *Stagestruck:Theater, AIDS and the Marketing of Gay America* (Duke University Press, 1998.)

LESLIE T. SHARPE is a writer, editor, and teacher. Her personal essays have appeared in *New York Newsday*, the *New York Times*, the *Village Voice*, the *Christian Science Monitor*, the *San Francisco Chronicle*, and the *Chicago Tribune*, among others. She is the author of E*diting Fact and Fiction: A Concise Guide to Book Editing*, published by Cambridge University Press in 1994. She currently teaches in the Writing Program of Columbia University (where she received her M.A. in Ancient Greek) and in the Certificate Program in Book Publishing of the City College of New York.

BOB SLAYMAKER'S poems have appeared in many literary reviews, including *Callaloo, Exquisite Corpse, Free Lunch, Gargoyle, Drumvoices Revue, River Styx, Weber Studies,* and *Zuzu's Petals Literary Quarterly.* His poems have also appeared in a number of newspapers and magazines, among them *The Christian Science Monitor, Interrace, The Omaha Star, The Orlando Times, Reggae Report, St. Anthony Messenger, The Charlotte Post,* and *Essence.* A product of MFA programs in writing and film at Columbia and NYU, he has taught at NYU, the State University of New York, Long Island University, the University of Hawaii, the City University of New York, and the University of California. He's been a featured reader at Barnes & Noble and Borders, and his work has been read on New York's WBAI-FM.

SUSAN THOMSEN, an editor of this issue, writes about theater for the online guide *New York Sidewalk*. She once shared an office at *The New Yorker* with a host of humorous colleagues, including the "Laughing Matters" co-editor, Betsey Osborne. Susan thanks Norman Trepner for making her laugh from the very beginning.

DEBRA WEINSTEIN is the author of *Rodent Angel* (NYU Press, 1996), a book of poetry. She is the recipient of a National Endowment for the Arts grant in poetry and a New York State Foundation for the Arts grant in fiction. *Mentor, Tormentor* is the first chapter of a novel in progress.

Upcoming Issues

Anything Can Happen—what's next for the new millenium, hopes and dreams, science fiction, miraculous events, disasters, history repeating itself, omens and prophecies, wishes, desires, predictions.

Secrets—keeping secrets and why, why not, secrets as taboo, secrets as intimacy, secrets and the unconscious, secrets in a confessional age, locks, doors and keys, passwords, handshakes and rituals, things you never told anyone.

You can subscribe to the newly-launched, larger *Global City Review*—lauded in a lengthy review in the *Los Angeles Times,* which looked at the history of literary magazines since Ezra Pound and concluded that *Global City Review* was "a better, more focused journal." *MultiCultural Review* also lent its praise, calling the review "a rich treasury of contemporary social thought and artistic expressions." With your support, *Global City Review* can continue to seek out and publish the most current, exciting, and provocative voices of today.

Global City Review is published annually.
Subscription Price: $6 for one year, $12 for two years
Institutions: $9 for one year, $18 for two years
International Price: $9 for one year, $18 for two years

Review Subscriptions can be paid by written check to:

Global City Review
Simon H. Rifkind Center for the Humanities
The City College of New York
138th and Convent Avenue
New York, NY 10031

Global City Backlist

All Global City Press publications are available at your local bookstore (in stock or by special order) or through our distributor, Consortium Book Sales & Distribution (1-800-283-3572).

GLOBAL CITY BOOKS

Ghost Stories, a story collection, $12.00, by E.M. Broner

House of Waiting, a novel, $12.00, by Marina Tamar Budhos

Safe House: Stories, a story collection, $12.00, by Burton Schulman

GLOBAL CITY ANTHOLOGIES

The Breast, $14.00, edited by Susan Thames and Marin Gazzaniga with Heather Ramsdell

Girls, $14.00, edited by Edith Chevat, Laurie Piette, and Angie Argabrite

GLOBAL CITY REVIEW (ALL $6.00)

Courting Danger, ISSUE TEN, Fall 1998

Every Picture Tells a Story, ISSUE NINE, Fall 1997

Fish Out of Water, ISSUE EIGHT, Fall 1996

Totem and Taboo, ISSUE SEVEN, Spring 1996

To Sleep! Perchance to Dream, ISSUE SIX, Fall 1995

Crime and Punishment, ISSUE FIVE, Spring 1995

To Make a Long Story Short, ISSUE FOUR, Fall 1994

Dr. Jekyll and Mr. Hyde, ISSUE THREE, Spring 1994

Paradise Lost, ISSUE TWO, Fall 1993

Sexual Politics, ISSUE ONE, Spring 1993